THE UNOFFICIAL
MASTERBUILT
ELECTRIC SMOKER
COOKBOOK

THE ART OF SMOKING MEAT
WITH YOUR ELECTRIC SMOKER

ROGER MURPHY

CONTENTS

INTRODUCTION

With clear and concise instructions, this book shows you how to get the most out of your smoker. This book provides detailed instructions on how to smoke meats, seafood, game, and vegetables, as well as tips on selecting the best cuts of meat and choosing the correct wood chips for flavor. Although the cookbook contains irresistible recipes guaranteed to please, including classic favorites like pulled pork and beef brisket, you'll also find exciting dishes like smoked chicken wings, tuna fillets, and even smoked gator ribs. Are you looking for a delicious way to add extra flavor to your meals? The sauces chapter is perfect for spicing up your dishes. Are you looking to perfect your smoked meat game? With beautiful photos and easy-to-follow steps, this book will help you take your smoking to the next level. Look no further than this fantastic masterbuilt electric smoker cookbook with everything you need to know about smoking meat, including how to choose the right smoker, what cuts of meat work best, and how to create flavorful recipes that impress you, your friends, and your family. Whether you're a beginner or a seasoned pro, this cookbook is a must-have for any smoker's library!

SMOKING

Smoking is generally used as one of the cooking methods nowadays. With modern cooking techniques, food enriched in protein, such as meat, would spoil if cooked for extended periods. Whereas, Smoking is a low & slow process of cooking meat. Where there is smoke, there is a flavor. With white smoke, you can boost the taste of your food. In addition to this statement, you can also preserve the nutrition in the food. Smoking is flexible & one of the oldest techniques of making food. You must brush the marinade over your food while you cook and let the miracle happen. The only thing you need to do is to add a handful of fresh wood chips when required. Just taste your regular grilled and smoked meat, and you will find the difference. Remember one thing, i.e., "Smoking is an art." With a bit of time & practice, even you can become an expert. Once you become an expert in smoking techniques, you will never look for other cooking techniques. To find which smoking technique works for you, you must experiment with different woods & cooking methods. Just cook the meat over an indirect heat source & cook it for hours. When smoking your meats, you must let the smoke escape & move around.

CHAPTER 1
BEEF

CUTS OF BEEF

(TOTAL COOK TIME 37 HOURS 30 MINUTES)

INGREDIENTS FOR 16 SERVINGS
THE MEAT

- Beef brisket (10-lbs, 4.5-kgs)

THE RUB

- Smoked paprika – ¼ cup
- White sugar – ¼ cup
- Brown sugar - ¼ cup
- Ground cumin – ¼ cup
- Cayenne pepper – ¼ cup
- Garlic powder – ¼ cup
- Chili powder – ¼ cup
- Onion powder – ¼ cup
- Sea salt – ¼ cup
- Freshly ground black pepper – ¼ cup

THE SMOKE

- While the smoker is cold, add your favorite wood chips to the wood tray
- Set the Masterbuilt smoker to 220-230°F (105-110°C)
- When the smoker has reached the desired temperature, put an additional batch of wood chips in the wood chip tray
- Fill the water pan to the level recommended in the smoker manual

METHOD

1. For the rub, in a bowl, combine the smoked paprika, white sugar, brown sugar, ground cumin, cayenne pepper, garlic powder, chili powder, onion powder, sea salt, and black pepper. Rub the mixture over the entire surface of the beef brisket. Transfer to the fridge for 24 hours.
2. Smoke the beef for approximately 12-13 hours or until it registers an internal temperature of 165°F (75°C). Wrap the beef tightly in aluminum foil and return to the smoker.
3. Continue to smoke the brisket for another 60 minutes or until it reaches an internal temperature of 185°F (85°C).

TEXAS-RUBBED BEEF BRISKET

(TOTAL COOK TIME 19 HOURS 20 MINUTES)

INGREDIENTS FOR 8 SERVINGS
THE MEAT

- Beef brisket, untrimmed (8-lbs, 4-kgs)

THE RUB

- Ancho chili powder- 3 tablespoons
- Sea salt – 2 tablespoons
- Ground allspice – 1 tablespoon
- Celery seeds – 1 tablespoon
- Garlic powder – 1 tablespoon
- Ground coriander seeds – 1 tablespoon
- Ground mustard seeds – 1 tablespoon
- Hungarian smoked paprika – 1 tablespoon
- Dried oregano – 1 tablespoon
- Freshly ground black pepper – 1 tablespoon
- Fresh apple juice– 2 cups
- Texas BBQ sauce, store-bought, of choice, warmed, as needed

13

THE SMOKE

- Before cooking, pre-soak 3 cups of pecan wood chips in water for 2-3 hours
- Set the Masterbuilt smoker to 220-230°F (105-110°C)
- When the smoker has reached the desired temperature, put an additional batch of wood chips in the wood chip tray
- Fill the water pan to the level recommended in the smoker manual

METHOD

1. First, prepare the rub. In a bowl, combine the Ancho chili powder, sea salt, allspice, celery seeds, garlic powder, coriander seeds, mustard seeds, smoked paprika, oregano, and black pepper.
2. Rub the spice mix over the beef brisket, cover tightly with kitchen wrap, and transfer to the fridge to chill overnight.
3. Around 60 minutes before you start to cook, allow the beef brisket to come to room temperature.
4. Place the brisket on the smoker grate fat side facing upwards and close the smoker.
5. Add the apple juice to a spray bottle.
6. Spray the meat with apple juice every 2 hours. Doing this will help to keep it moist.
7. After around 4 hours, or when the internal temperature of the beef registers 165°F (75°C), wrap the brisket in aluminum foil and cook for an additional 4 hours.
8. When the beef registers an internal temperature of 185°F (85°C), remove from the smoker and set aside for 15-20 minutes before slicing.
9. Serve the beef brisket with your choice of warmed Texas BBQ sauce and enjoy.

(TOTAL COOK TIME 9 HOURS 15 MINUTES)

INGREDIENTS FOR 4 SERVINGS
THE MEAT

- 4-bone section beef ribs (4-lb, 1.8-kg)

THE INGREDIENTS

- Horseradish flavor Dijon mustard, any brand – 2 tablespoons
- Beef rub, any brand – 6 tablespoons

THE SPRITZ

- Hot sauce, any brand – ¼ cup
- White vinegar - 1 cup'

THE SMOKE

- Add Hickory or oak wood chips to the wood tray.
- Set the Masterbuilt smoker to 250°F (120°C) for indirect cooking
- When the smoker has reached the desired temperature, put an additional batch of wood chips in the wood chip tray
- Fill the water pan to the level recommended in the smoker manual

METHOD

1. Cover the beef ribs with the flavored mustard, and season generously all over with beef rub.
2. Transfer the ribs to the preheated smoker, and insert a meat thermometer, programmed to 200°F (95°C) in the thickest part of the ribs while not touching the bone. Close the smoker's lid and smoke the ribs for 3 hours.
3. Add the hot sauce and white vinegar to a spray bottle and shake to combine.
4. Once the ribs have smoked for 3 hours, start to spritz them every 40-60 minutes. Continue to smoke until they register an internal temperature of 200°F (95°C). The whole smoking process will take approximately 8-10 hours.
5. Take the beef ribs out of the smoker and wrap them in aluminum foil. Set aside to rest in an insulated cooler for a minimum of 60 minutes before slicing.
6. Enjoy.

SMOKED BEEF RIBS WITH TEXAS RED BBQ SAUCE

(TOTAL COOK TIME 3 HOURS 15 MINUTES)

INGREDIENTS FOR 4-6 SERVINGS
THE MEAT

- 1 slab beef back ribs

THE DRY RUB

- Chili powder – 1 tablespoon
- Garlic powder – 1 teaspoon
- Cumin – ½ teaspoon
- Thyme – ¼ teaspoon

THE RED SAUCE

- Ketchup – 2 ½ cups
- Cider vinegar – ¾ cup
- Red wine vinegar – ¾ cup
- Brown sugar - ⅓ cup
- Worcestershire sauce - ⅓ cup
- Hot sauce – ¼ cup
- Water - ⅓ cup
- Chili powder – 3½ tablespoons
- Cumin – 1¼ tablespoons
- Allspice – ½ teaspoon
- Garlic powder – 2 teaspoons
- Salt – ¾ tablespoon
- Black pepper – 2 tablespoons

THE SMOKE

- While the smoker is cold, add your favorite wood chips to the wood tray
- Set the Masterbuilt smoker to 250°F (120°C)
- When the smoker has reached the desired temperature, put an additional batch of wood chips in the wood chip tray
- Fill the water pan to the level recommended in the smoker manual

METHOD

1. Combine the rub ingredients (chili powder, garlic powder, cumin, and thyme).
2. Clean the ribs and remove the membrane. With a knife, loosen the membrane and, using a paper towel, peel back. Season the ribs on both sides liberally with dry rub.
3. Smoke the ribs for 2½ -3 hours until the meat registers 200°F (95°C) in the middle. Remove from the smoker and rest for 15 minutes.
4. Meanwhile, prepare the red sauce. In a bowl, combine the ketchup, cider vinegar, red wine vinegar, brown sugar, Worcestershire sauce, hot sauce, water, chili powder, cumin, allspice, garlic powder, salt, and black pepper. Serve with the Texas Red sauce and enjoy.

(TOTAL COOK TIME 2 HOURS)

INGREDIENTS FOR 8 SERVINGS
THE MEAT

- Tri-tip steak beef, patted dry (3-lbs, 1.4-kgs)

THE INGREDIENTS

- Kosher salt – 3 tablespoons
- Freshly ground black pepper – 3 tablespoons

THE SMOKE

- While the smoker is cold, add oak wood chips to the wood tray
- Set the Masterbuilt smoker for indirect cooking to 225°F (110°C)
- When the smoker has reached the desired temperature, put an additional batch of wood chips in the wood chip tray
- Fill the water pan to the level recommended in the smoker manual

METHOD

1. Rub the meat all over with salt and pepper.
2. Smoke for 60-90 minutes until the meat registers an internal temperature of 130°F (55°C).
3. Remove the meat from the smoker and wrap tightly in parchment paper. Return the meat to the smoker and cook for an additional 30-60 minutes until it registers at an internal temperature of 140°F (60°C).
4. Remove the meat from the smoker and set aside for 20 minutes before slicing against the grain.
5. Serve and enjoy.

(TOTAL COOK TIME 10 HOURS 20 MINUTES)

INGREDIENTS FOR 2 SERVINGS
THE MEAT

- Oxtails (4-lbs, 1.8-kgs)

THE INGREDIENTS

- Jerk marinade, store-bought, of choice – ¼ cup
- Apple cider vinegar – 2 tablespoons

THE SMOKE

- Add Hickory or oak wood chips to the wood tray.
- Set the Masterbuilt smoker to 250°F (120°C) for indirect cooking
- When the smoker has reached the desired temperature, put an additional batch of wood chips in the wood chip tray
- Fill the water pan to the level recommended in the smoker manual

METHOD

1. Add the oxtails to a bowl.
2. Rub the oxtails all over with the jerk marinade. Cover the bowl and place it in the fridge overnight to marinade.
3. Smoke the oxtail for 2 hours.
4. Add the apple cider vinegar to a spray bottle. Open the smoker and spritz the oxtail with apple cider vinegar.
5. Continue to smoke the oxtail for an additional 2-3 hours until the meat registers an internal temperature of 180°F (80°C). Spritz the oxtail with apple cider vinegar as it smokes. Doing this will help to keep the meat moist.
6. Take the meat out of the smoker and allow to rest for 12-15 minutes before serving.

(TOTAL COOK TIME 1 HOUR 45 MINUTES)

INGREDIENTS FOR 4 SERVINGS
THE MEAT

- Lean minced beef (8-ozs, 230-gms)
- Minced pork (8-ozs, 230-gms)

THE INGREDIENTS

- 1 medium onion (peeled and finely diced)
- Breadcrumbs – ¼ cup
- Garlic powder – 1 teaspoon
- Tomato paste – 2 tablespoons
- 1 egg, beaten
- Pinch salt

THE MASH

- Starchy potatoes, scrubbed and diced (2-lbs, 0.9-kgs)
- Kosher salt, as needed
- Whole milk – 1 cup
- Butter – 3 tablespoons
- Sour cream – ⅔ cup
- Cheddar cheese, grated – ½ cup

THE TOPPINGS

- 5 slices bacon, cooked and chopped
- Diced tomato
- Spring onions, thinly sliced
- Chives, thinly sliced

THE SMOKE

- While the smoker is cold, add mesquite wood chips to the wood tray
- Set the Masterbuilt smoker to 250°F (120°C)
- When the smoker has reached the desired temperature, put an additional batch of wood chips in the wood chip tray
- Fill the water pan to the level recommended in the smoker manual

METHOD

1. In a bowl, combine the minced beef, minced pork, onion, breadcrumbs, garlic powder, tomato paste, egg, and salt until incorporated. Press the meat mixture into the bottom of a lightly greased casserole or pie dish to create a crust.
2. Transfer to the smoker for around 60 minutes until cooked through.
3. In the meantime, add the potatoes to a large saucepan. Pour in sufficient water to cover and season with salt. Bring the potatoes to a boil, and then uncovered, simmer for 10-12 minutes.
4. Heat the milk with the butter gently in a small pan, and set aside until the potatoes are cooked through.
5. Strain the potatoes and place in a bowl. Mash the potatoes until fluffy and add the sour cream. Whisk in the milk and butter mixture until creamy.
6. Remove the baking dish from the smoker and spread the mash evenly over the top.
7. Sprinkle over the grated Cheddar cheese and return to the smoker for an additional 15-20 minutes until the cheese melts and crisps.
8. Top the pie with the chopped bacon, diced tomatoes, spring onions, and chives. Enjoy.

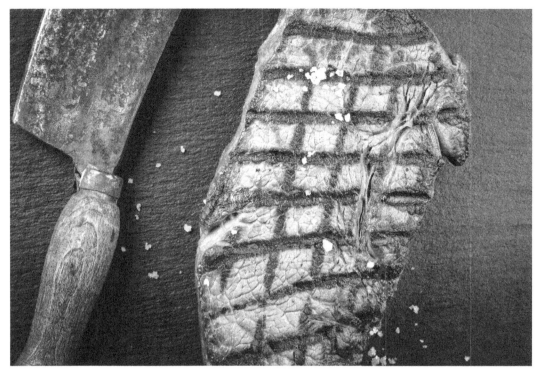

(TOTAL COOK TIME 1 HOUR 30 MINUTES)

INGREDIENTS FOR 2 SERVINGS
THE MEAT

- 2 New York strip steaks

THE BUTTER

- Salted butter, room temperature – ½ cup
- Fresh parsley, chopped – 1 tablespoon
- 1 green onion top, minced
- Bourbon – 2 tablespoons
- Smoked paprika – 1 teaspoon

THE SEASONING

- Steak rub

THE SMOKE

- Preheat the electric smoker to 225°f (110°c) using pecan wood chips
- When the smoker has reached the desired temperature, put an additional batch of wood chips in the wood chip tray
- Fill the water pan to the level recommended in the smoker manual

METHOD

1. First, prepare the butter. Combine the butter, parsley, green onion, bourbon, and paprika in a small bowl. Transfer to a piece of plastic wrap, shape into a log and roll tightly. Chill until ready to use.
2. Season the steaks with steak rub and place in the smoker. Cook for approximately 60 minutes until the internal temperature registers 130°f (55°c), for medium-rare.
3. Place a skillet over high heat. When the steak is cooked to your liking, sear each piece on both sides in the skillet.
4. Top with a couple slices of bourbon butter and serve straight away.

CHAPTER 2
PORK

CUTS ⚏ PORK

(TOTAL COOK TIME 30 HOUR 20 MINUTES)

INGREDIENTS FOR 2-3 SERVINGS
THE MEAT

- 1 rack pork spareribs (3-4-lbs, 1.4-1.8-kgs)

THE BRINE

- Coarse sea salt – ¾ cup
- Pink curing salt – 1½ teaspoons
- Honey – ¾ cup
- Hot water – 3 cups
- 8 whole cloves
- 3 bay leaves

THE SMOKE

- While the smoker is cold, add your choice of wood chips to the wood tray
- Set the Masterbuilt smoker for indirect cooking to 225-250°F (105-110C).
- When the smoker has reached the desired temperature, put an additional batch of wood chips in the wood chip tray
- Fill the water pan to the level recommended in the smoker manual

METHOD

1. Arrange the ribs on a chopping board. Remove and discard the membrane from the back of each rack. Widthwise, cut each rack in half between the middle bones. Transfer the ribs to an extra-large ziplock bag.
2. For the brine: Combine the salt, pink curing salt with the honey, and hot water and whisk until the ingredients are dissolved. Whisk in the cold water and add the whole cloves followed by the bay leaves. Set aside to cool to room temperature.
3. Pour the brine over the ribs in the bag, and expel the air. Seal the bag and place in a roasting pan. Transfer to the fridge to brine for 1 day, turning the bag over 2 times a day to ensure an even cure.
4. The following day, drain the ribs thoroughly and discard the brine. Pat the ribs dry with kitchen paper towels.
5. Place the ribs on a wire rack set over a rimmed baking sheet and allow to dry for 2 hours in the fridge.
6. Put the ribs directly on the smoker's rack with the bone side facing downwards and smoke for 4-5 hours, until pull-apart tender.
7. Serve hot and enjoy.

(TOTAL COOK TIME 6 HOUR 15 MINUTES)

INGREDIENTS FOR 16 SERVINGS
THE MEAT

- Pork butt roast, brined (7-lbs, 3.2-kgs)

THE RUB

- Ground chili powder – 2 tablespoons
- Packed brown sugar – 4 tablespoons

THE SMOKE

- While the smoker is cold, add your choice of wood chips to the wood tray
- Set the Masterbuilt smoker for indirect cooking to 200-225°F (105-110°C).
- When the smoker has reached the desired temperature, put an additional batch of wood chips in the wood chip tray
- Fill the water pan to the level recommended in the smoker manual

METHOD

1. In a bowl, combine the brown sugar with the chili powder. Using clean hands, rub the mixture all over the meat.
2. Set a roasting rack in a drip pan.
3. Place the meat on the rack and smoke for 6-8 hours until the meat registers an internal temperature of 145°F (65°C).
4. Serve and enjoy.

(TOTAL COOK TIME 9 HOURS)

INGREDIENTS FOR 3 SERVINGS
THE MEAT

- 3 bone-in pork chops (1.5-ins, 4 cms) thick

THE BRINE

- Apple cider – 1 cup
- Kosher salt - ⅓ cup
- 4 black peppercorns
- Brown sugar – 2 tablespoons
- 3 garlic cloves, peeled and smashed
- Fresh thyme

THE SEASONING

- Sea salt – ½ tablespoon
- Freshly ground black pepper – ½ tablespoon
- Smoked paprika – ½ tablespoon
- Ground garlic – 1 teaspoon

THE SMOKE

- While the smoker is cold, add your choice of wood chips to the wood tray.
- Set the Masterbuilt smoker for indirect cooking to 250°F (120°C). When the smoker has reached the desired temperature, put an additional batch of wood chips in the wood chip tray
- Fill the water pan to the level recommended in the smoker manual

METHOD

1. First, brine the pork. Add the apple cider, kosher salt, black peppercorns, brown sugar, garlic, and fresh herbs to a bowl. Add the chops to the brine and place in the fridge overnight.
2. The following day and using a kitchen paper towel, pat dry and season with salt, black pepper, paprika, and ground garlic. Set the chops aside to come to room temperature.
3. Smoke for 45 minutes until they reach an internal temperature of 145°F (65°C).
4. Enjoy.

PULLED PORK

(TOTAL COOK TIME 20 HOURS 40 MINUTES)

INGREDIENTS FOR 20 SERVINGS
THE MEAT

- Pork shoulder roast (8-lbs, 3.7-kgs)
- Apple cider vinegar, as needed

THE RUB

- White sugar – 5 tablespoons
- Light brown sugar – 5 tablespoons
- Sea salt – 2 tablespoons
- Smoked paprika – 2 tablespoons
- Onion powder – 1 tablespoon
- Freshly ground black pepper – 1 tablespoon
- Garlic powder – 1 tablespoon
- 1 onion, peeled and chopped

THE SMOKE

- While the smoker is cold, add 3 cups of pre-soaked hickory wood chips to the wood tray
- Set the Masterbuilt smoker for indirect cooking to 275°F (135°C).
- When the smoker has reached the desired temperature, put an additional batch of wood chips in the wood chip tray
- Fill the water pan with the cider brine and to the level recommended in the smoker manual and replenish as necessary

METHOD

1. Put the meat in a large pot, and pour in sufficient apple cider to cover.
2. For the rub, in a bowl, combine the white and brown sugars, salt, smoked paprika, onion powder, black pepper, and garlic powder. Mix approximately ¼ cup of the sugar rub into the cider. Set the remaining rub aside.
3. Cover the pot and transfer to the fridge for 12 hours.
4. Pour the cider brine into the smoker's water pan. Add the onion along with an additional ¼ cup more of sugar rub.
5. Spread the remaining rub over the meat and place in the middle of the smoker.
6. Smoke the pork for 8 hours, until tender.
7. Transfer the pork to a serving platter and cool for half an hour before shredding with metal forks.
8. Serve and enjoy.

SMOKED HAM WITH BROWN SUGAR GLAZE

(TOTAL COOK TIME 4 HOURS 10 MINUTES)

INGREDIENTS FOR 8-10 SERVINGS

THE MEAT

- 1 bone-in ham (7-lb, 3.2-kg)

THE INGREDIENTS

- Nonstick cooking spray
- BBQ rub, any brand – ⅓ cup
- Apple cider, divided – 2¼ cups
- Fresh herbs, of choice, to garnish, optional
- Fresh fruit, of choice, to garnish, optional

THE GLAZE

- Butter – ½ cup
- Brown sugar – ½ cup
- Maple syrup – ¼ cup

THE SMOKE

- Cherry wood chips are a good choice for this recipe
- Set the Masterbuilt smoker for indirect cooking to 250°F (120°C).
- When the smoker has reached the desired temperature, put an additional batch of wood chips in the wood chip tray
- Fill the water pan with the cider brine and to the level recommended in the smoker manual and replenish as necessary

METHOD

1. Coat an aluminum foil pan with nonstick cooking spray.
2. Lay the ham, cut side facing down in the foil pan.
3. Scatter the BBQ rub over the surface of the meant.
4. Transfer the foil pan to the smoker and cook for 60 minutes.
5. Continue cooking the ham for an additional 2-3 hours, basting every 30-40 minutes with the 2 cups of cider. The ham is good to go when it registers an internal temperature of 140°F (60°C).
6. Meanwhile, prepare the glaze. Over moderate heat, combine the butter, brown sugar, syrup, and remaining apple cider in a pan. Bring to a simmer and cook until the glaze has thickened, for 6-8 minutes.
7. Brush the glaze over the surface of the ham. Transfer to a platter and garnish with herbs and fresh fruit.
8. Enjoy.

PEACH BARBECUE PULLED PORK

(TOTAL COOK TIME 5 HOURS 15 MINUTES)

INGREDIENTS FOR 20 SERVINGS
THE MEAT

- Pork shoulder (10-lb, 4.5-kg)

THE INGREDIENTS

- Pork rub, any brand – 1 cup
- Peach BBQ sauce, any brand, as needed
- 20 sandwich buns, split
- Coleslaw, as needed

THE SMOKE

- Set the Masterbuilt smoker for indirect cooking to 250-275°F (120-135°C)
- Hickory or pecan wood chips work well for this recipe
- When the smoker has reached the desired temperature, put an additional batch of wood chips in the wood chip tray
- Fill the water pan with the cider brine and to the level recommended in the smoker manual and replenish as necessary

METHOD

1. Using kitchen paper towels, pat the meat dry.
2. Take a sharp knife and make cuts all over the surface of the butt. Scatter the pork rub over the pork, pressing it gently into the meat.
3. Cook the meat on indirect cooking at around 250-275°F (120-135°C).
4. Cook the pork for around 5 hours, or until the internal temperature of the meat registers an internal temperature of 195-205°F (90-95°C) until the meat falls apart.
5. Remove from the smoker and set aside to rest for 20 minutes before shredding.
6. Mix 10 cups of sauce into the pulled, shredded pork.
7. Cook until heated through.
8. Serve the pulled pork in the sandwich buns topped with coleslaw.
9. Enjoy.

APPLE SMOKED PORK TENDERLOIN

(TOTAL COOK TIME 6 HOURS 45 MINUTES)

INGREDIENTS FOR 4-6 SERVINGS
THE MEAT

- 2 pork tenderloins (2-lbs, 0.9-kgs) each

THE MARINADE

- Runny honey, warm – 3 tablespoons
- Fresh apple juice – ½ cup
- Pork rub, store-bought, of choice – 3 tablespoons
- Brown sugar – ¼ cup
- Thyme leaves – 2 tablespoons
- Freshly ground black pepper – ½ teaspoon

THE SMOKE

- When you are ready to cook, preheat your Masterbuilt smoker to 225°F (110°C) for 12-15 minutes
- Applewood wood chips are recommended for this recipe
- When the smoker has reached the desired temperature, put an additional batch of wood chips in the wood chip tray
- Fill the water pan with the cider brine and to the level recommended in the smoker manual and replenish as necessary

METHOD

1. For the marinade: In a bowl, combine the honey, apple juice, pork rub, brown sugar, thyme, and black pepper, and whisk well to incorporate.
2. Add the pork tenderloins to the marinade, turning until evenly and well coat. Cover the bowl with plastic wrap and transfer to the refrigerator for 2-3 hours to marinate.
3. Place the meat directly on the grate and smoke until the pork registers an internal temperature of 145°F (65°C) for 2½-3 hours.
4. Set aside for 6-8 minutes before slicing.
5. Enjoy.

RIBS WITH WARM MUSTARD POTATO SALAD

(TOTAL COOK TIME 5 HOURS 45 MINUTES)

INGREDIENTS FOR 6 SERVINGS
THE MEAT

- Pork ribs (3-lbs, 1.35-kgs)

THE RUB

- Salt – ½ tablespoon
- Brown sugar – ¼ cup
- Chili powder- 2½ teaspoons
- Cayenne pepper – 2 teaspoons
- Ground cumin – 1½ tablespoons
- Freshly ground black pepper – 2 teaspoon
- Onion powder – 2 teaspoons
- Garlic powder – 2 teaspoons

THE POTATO SALAD

- Small red potatoes (2-lbs, 0.9-kgs)
- Full-fat mayonnaise – 1 cup
- Dijon mustard – ¼ cup
- Red onion, peeled and chopped 0 ½ cup
- 2 green onions with tops, sliced
- 2 cloves of garlic, peeled and minced
- Fresh dill, snipped – 3 tablespoons
- Salt – ½ teaspoon
- Black pepper – ½ teaspoon
- Freshly squeezed lime juice – ¼ teaspoon

THE SMOKE

- Preheat your electric smoker to 225°F (110°C)
- Add hickory wood chips to the smoker

METHOD

1. In a bowl, combine the salt with the brown sugar, chili powder, cayenne pepper, cumin, black pepper, onion powder, and garlic powder.
2. Rub the mixture all over the pork ribs and put aside for 2 hours to allow the meat to come to room temperature.
3. Smoke the pork ribs in the smoker for 2 hours with the hickory chips. Continue smoking for another 60 minutes with no hickory wood chips.
4. Remove the ribs from the smoker and wrap in aluminum foil.
5. Return the ribs to the smoker and continue smoking for another 60-90 minutes.
6. In the meantime, prepare the potato salad.
7. Add the potatoes to a pan and pour in sufficient water to cover. Bring to boil and cook for 20-25 minutes, until tender. Drain and allow to cool.
8. In a bowl, combine the remaining ingredients (mayonnaise, mustard, red onion, green onion, garlic, dill, salt, pepper, and lime juice.
9. Cut the cooled potatoes into bite-sized chunks, add them to the bowl, and toss to evenly coat.Serve the ribs with the potato salad and enjoy.

(TOTAL COOK TIME 50 HOURS 25 MINUTES)

INGREDIENTS FOR 12 SERVINGS
THE MEAT

- 6 ham hocks

THE BRINE

- Filtered water, boiling (2-gl, 8-qts)
- Brown sugar – 1 cup
- Salt – 2 cups
- Black peppercorns – 2 teaspoons
- 4 bay leaves

THE SMOKE

- Add hickory flavor wood chips to the wood tray
- Set the Masterbuilt smoker to 250°F (120°C)
- When the smoker has reached the desired temperature, put an additional batch of wood chips in the wood chip tray
- Fill the water pan to the level recommended in the smoker manual

METHOD

1. First, prepare the brine. In a deep saucepan, combine the boiling water with brown sugar, salt, peppercorns, and bay leaves. Stir the brine thoroughly to dissolve the brown sugar and salt entirely. Set the brine aside to cool.
2. Add the ham hocks to large ziplock bags, and put the bags in a dish.
3. Pour an even amount of brine into each bag, and securely seal. Transfer to the refrigerator for one day.
4. Remove the hocks from the brine, rinse well, and using a kitchen paper towel, pat dry.
5. Put a rack inside a roasting pan.
6. Place the ham hocks on the rack and transfer them to the fridge to chill for another day.
7. Place the ham hocks in the smoker, smoke for 2-4 hours.
8. The ham hocks are ready to serve when they register an internal temperature of 160° F (70°C).

CHAPTER 3
LAMB

CUTS OF LAMB

PULLED LAMB SHOULDER

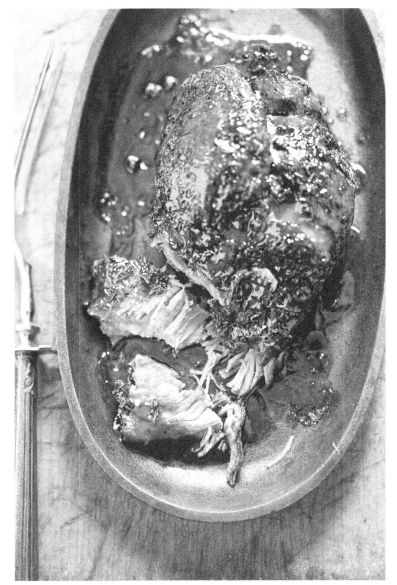

(TOTAL COOK TIME 6 HOURS 20 MINUTES)

INGREDIENTS FOR 10-12 SERVINGS
THE MEAT

- 1 bone-in lamb shoulder (10-lbs, 4.5-kgs)

THE INGREDIENTS

- Packed dark brown sugar – ¾ cup
- Kosher salt – ½ cup
- Ground espresso beans – ½ cup
- Cracked black pepper – 2 tablespoons
- Garlic powder – 2 teaspoons
- Ground cinnamon – 1 tablespoon
- Ground cumin – 1 tablespoon
- Cayenne pepper – 1 tablespoon
- Hamburger buns, to serve

THE SAUCE

- Worcestershire sauce – ½ cup
- Stout – ½ cup
- White vinegar – ½ cup
- Ketchup – 1 tablespoon
- Freshly squeezed lemon juice – 2 teaspoons
- Dark brown sugar – 3 tablespoons
- Kosher salt – 1 teaspoon
- Cracked black pepper – ½ teaspoon
- Ground allspice – ¼ teaspoons
- Onion powder – ¼ teaspoon
- Garlic powder – ¼ teaspoon

THE SMOKER

- Add wood chips of your choise to the wood tray
- Preheat the electric smoker to 225°F (110°C)
- When the smoker has reached the desired temperature, put an additional batch of wood chips in the wood chip tray
- Fill the water pan to the level recommended in the smoker manual

METHOD

1. Place the lamb on a rimmed baking pan and put to one side.
2. For the rub: In a bowl, combine the sugar with the salt, espresso beans, pepper, garlic powder, cinnamon, cumin and cayenne and stir thoroughly to incorporate. Aim to yield 2 cups.
3. Use around half of the rub to all the lamb all over. Make sure you rub it into all the meat crevices. Set the remaining rub to one side.
4. Put the lamb in the smoker and smoke at between 225°-250°F (110°-120°C). You may need to replenish the wood chips as necessary.
5. After 4 hours of smoking, check on the lamb's progress every 20 minutes. The lamb is sufficiently cooked when it registers 185°F (85°C) when using an internal thermometer. This will take around 6 hours.
6. Transfer the lamb to a clean rimmed sheet pan and put to one side to rest.
7. In the meantime, prepare the sauce. In a pan over moderate heat, combine 1 ½ cups of water with the remaining ingredients (Worcestershire sauce, stout, vinegar, ketchup, lemon juice, brown sugar, kosher salt, black pepper, allspice, onion powder, and garlic powder). Stir well to incorporate.
8. Bring the sauce to boil before reducing the heat and allowing it to slightly thicken, for 5-7 minutes. Remove the pan from the heat and set aside to cool.
9. Using kitchen tongs, pull the lamb apart while removing and discarding any larger pieces of fat.
10. Once all the lamb has been pulled, add additional rub to taste, and stir well to incorporate.
11. Serve with the hamburger buns and serve the sauce on the side.

MAPLE SMOKED LAMB SHANKS

(TOTAL COOK TIME 28 HOURS 10 MINUTES)

INGREDIENTS FOR 10-12 SERVINGS
THE MEAT

- 10-12 lamb shanks

THE MARINADE

- Bourbon (4-ozs, 110-gms)
- Dry red wine - 1¾ cups
- Garlic, peeled, and minced – 1 tablespoon
- Rosemary – 2 tablespoons
- Salt and freshly ground black pepper

THE SMOKE

- While the smoker is cold, add maple wood chips to the wood tray.
- Set the Masterbuilt smoker to 225°F (110°C)
- When the smoker has reached the desired temperature, put an additional batch of wood chips in the wood chip tray
- Fill the water pan to the level recommended in the smoker manual
- Lightly oil a smoker rack

METHOD

1. Prepare the marinade: Combine the bourbon with red wine, garlic, and rosemary. Mix well and season with salt and pepper.
2. Add the lamb shanks to a baking dish.
3. Pour the marinade over the meat, and cover with a lid.
4. Transfer the dish to the fridge for 24 hours. You will need to turn the meat occasionally during this time to ensure an even marinade.
5. Remove the lamb from the marinade, shake off any excess, and place on the smoker rack.
6. Smoke the lamb for around 4 hours or until cooked to your preferred level of doneness.

(TOTAL COOK TIME 11 HOURS 30 MINUTES)

INGREDIENTS FOR 4 SERVINGS
THE MEAT

- Lamb neck (2-lb, 0.9-kg)

THE BRINE

- Water – 8 cups
- Kosher salt – ½ cup

THE DRY RUB

- Dried rosemary – 1 tablespoon
- Dried thyme – 1 tablespoon
- Ground black pepper – 1 teaspoon
- Garlic salt – 1 teaspoon

THE SMOKE

- While the smoker is cold, add hickory wood chips to the wood tray.
- Set the Masterbuilt smoker to 250°F (120°C)
- When the smoker has reached the desired temperature, put an additional batch of wood chips in the wood chip tray
- Fill the water pan to the level recommended in the smoker manual
- Lightly oil a smoker rack

METHOD

1. For the wet brine, add the water and salt to a bucket, and stir until the salt dissolves.
2. Place the lamb in the bucket and submerge in the brine. Transfer the bucket to the fridge and leave overnight.
3. The following day remove the meat from the brine and rinse with cold water. Pat dry with kitchen paper towels.
4. Slice the lamb into steaks on less than 0.5-in (1.5-cm) thick.
5. Mix the dry rub ingredients (dried rosemary, thyme, black pepper, and salt) in a bowl. Crush any lumps with a fork.
6. Apply a liberal amount of the rub over the lamb, covering on all sides and into any folds.
7. Place the lamb on your smoker's grates and smoke the lamb for around 2½ hours until the meat registers an internal temperature of 145°F (65°C).
8. Remove the lamb from the smoker and tent it loosely in foil. Set aside to rest for 20-30 minutes.
9. Serve and enjoy.

SMOKED RACK OF LAMB WITH BUTTER PASTE

(TOTAL COOK TIME 1 HOUR 45 MINUTES)

INGREDIENTS FOR 2 SERVINGS
THE MEAT

- 1 whole rack of lamb

THE SEASONING

- Olive oil – 2 tablespoons
- Salt and black pepper, as needed

THE HERB BUTTER PASTE

- Butter – ¼ cup
- Olive oil – 2 tablespoons
- Fresh parsley, chopped – 2 tablespoons
- Cumin – 1 tablespoon
- Garlic, peeled and minced – 1 tablespoon
- Salt and freshly ground black pepper, to season

THE SMOKE

- While the smoker is cold, add hickory or apple wood chips to the wood tray.
- Set the Masterbuilt smoker to 225°F (110°C)
- When the smoker has reached the desired temperature, put an additional batch of wood chips in the wood chip tray
- Fill the water pan to the level recommended in the smoker manual
- Lightly oil a smoker rack

METHOD

1. In a bowl, combine the herb paste ingredients (butter, olive oil, parsley, cumin, and garlic). Season with salt and black pepper.
2. Rub olive oil over the lamb rack and season with salt and black pepper. On the bone-free side, rub the paste evenly all over the meat.
3. Place the lamb in the smoker for 90 minutes until the internal temperature registers 225°F (110°C).
4. When the lamb is ready, remove it from the smoker and sear quickly on both sides, for 60 seconds each.
5. Allow the lamb to rest for 10 minutes before serving.

SMOKED LEG OF LAMB

(TOTAL COOK TIME 2 HOURS 30 MINUTES)

INGREDIENTS FOR 8 SERVINGS
THE MEAT

- 1 leg of lamb, bone-in (5-lb, 2.25-kg)

THE GARLIC AND HERB PASTE

- Olive oil – 1 cup
- Freshly squeezed lemon juice – 6 tablespoons
- Dijon mustard – ¼ cup
- 10 whole garlic cloves, peeled
- 12 sprigs of rosemary
- 12 sprigs of thyme
- 4 shallots
- Sea salt – ½ cup
- Freshly ground black pepper – 2 tablespoons

THE SMOKE

- While the smoker is cold, add cherry or apple wood chips to the wood tray.
- Set the Masterbuilt smoker to 250°F (120°C)
- When the smoker has reached the desired temperature, put an additional batch of wood chips in the wood chip tray
- Fill the water pan to the level recommended in the smoker manual

METHOD

1. Combine the olive oil with fresh lemon juice, Dijon mustard, garlic, rosemary sprigs, thyme sprigs, shallots, salt, and black pepper in a food blender or a processor. Process to a semi-liquid paste consistency.
2. Brush the mixture over the lamb to cover it entirely.
3. Transfer the lamb to the smoker, and cook for 2-3 hours, or until the meat registers 145°F (65°C).
4. Remove the meat from the smoker and cover loosely with foil. Allow the meat to rest for around 25-35 minutes before slicing

SMOKED LAMB LOIN CHOPS WITH CREAMY FETA SAUCE

(TOTAL COOK TIME 2 HOURS 10 MINUTES)

INGREDIENTS FOR 4-8 SERVINGS
THE MEAT

- 8 lamb loin chops

THE INGREDIENTS

- Pesto – ⅔ cup

THE SAUCE

- Cream 10% - ¼ cup
- Feta cheese – ½ cup
- Olive oil – 1 tablespoon
- Salt – ½ teaspoon
- Black pepper – ½ teaspoon

THE SMOKE

- While the smoker is cold, add cherry or apple wood chips to the wood tray.
- Set the Masterbuilt smoker to 250°F (120°C)
- When the smoker has reached the desired temperature, put an additional batch of wood chips in the wood chip tray
- Fill the water pan to the level recommended in the smoker manual

METHOD

1. In a bowl, toss the lamb chops with the pesto to evenly coat. Cover with kitchen wrap and place in the refrigerator for a minimum of 60 minutes to marinate.
2. Arrange the lamb chops on the smoker rack in the smoker and smoke for approximately 2 hours until the meat registers an internal temperature of 145°F (65°C).
3. In the meantime, prepare the sauce: Add the cream, feta, oil, salt, and black pepper to a blender jar and process until creamy smooth. You may need to add a drop more cream to thin the sauce a little, if necessary.
4. Remove the chops from the smoker and serve with the feta sauce.

SMOKED BONELESS LEG OF LAMB

(TOTAL COOK TIME 4 HOURS 20 MINUTES)

INGREDIENTS FOR 4 SERVINGS
THE MEAT

- 1 boneless leg of lamb, fat trimmed (2-lbs, 0.9-kgs)

THE RUB

- 4 cloves of garlic, peeled and minced
- Salt – 2 tablespoons
- Freshly ground black pepper – 1 tablespoon
- Oregano – 2 tablespoons
- Thyme – 1 teaspoon
- Olive oil – 2 tablespoons

THE SMOKE

- Preheat your electric smoker to 250°F (120°C)
- Apple, hickory or oak wood chips are recommended for this recipe

METHOD

1. Once the meat is trimmed, attempt to keep the lamb an even thickness. Doing this will help to achieve an even cook. You can tie the meat up using kitchen twine to create a roast if required.
2. In a bowl, combine the garlic with the salt, black pepper, oregano, thyme, and oil. Rub the seasoning all over the meat.
3. Place the meat on a platter and cover with kitchen wrap. Transfer to the fridge for at least 60 minutes to marinate.
4. Remove the meat from the fridge, shake off any excess marinade, and place it on a smoker rack.
5. Smoke the meat for 3-4 hours until, for medium-rare, it registers an internal temperature of 145°F (65°C).
6. Once the meat is cooked to your preference, remove it from the smoker. Set aside to cool a little and slice.

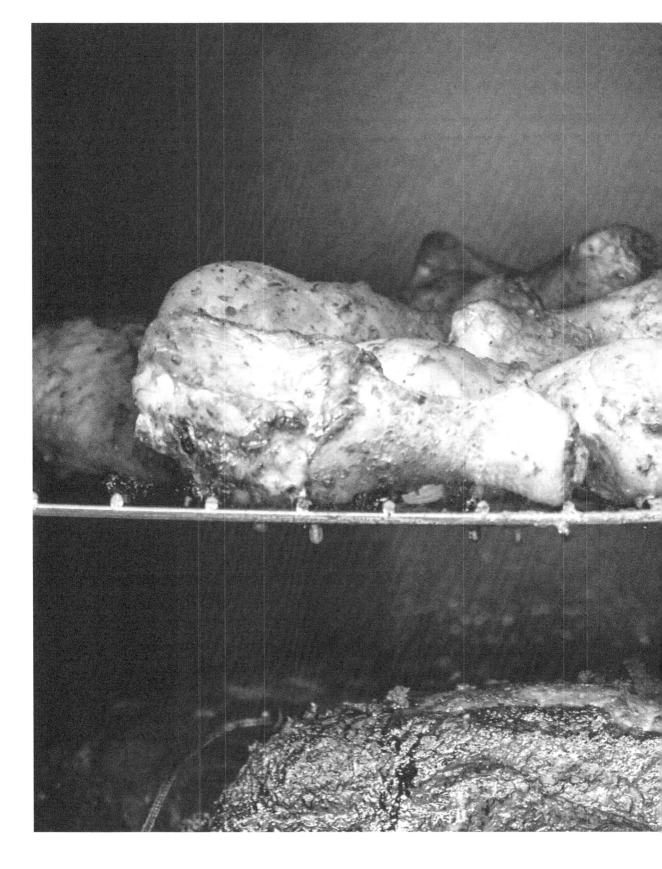

CHAPTER 4
POULTRY

CUTS ⸺ OF ⸺ TURKEY

CHERRY COLA CHICKEN WINGS

(TOTAL COOK TIME 20 HOURS 20 MINUTES)

INGREDIENTS FOR 12 SERVINGS
THE MEAT

- Chicken wings, partitioned, tips discarded (4-lb, 1.8-kg)

THE BRINE

- Cherry cola – 4¼ cups
- Kosher salt – 2 tablespoons

THE INGREDIENTS

- BBQ rub – 4 tablespoons
- Brown sugar – 4 tablespoons
- Cornstarch – 4 tablespoons

THE SMOKE

- Add your favorite wood chips to the wood tray
- Preheat the Masterbuilt smoker to 150°F (65°C)
- When the smoker has reached the desired temperature, put an additional batch of wood chips in the wood chip tray
- Fill the water pan to the level recommended in the smoker manual

METHOD

1. Around 18 hours before you cook the wings, add them to a ziplock bag.
2. Pour in the cherry cola and 2 tablespoons of kosher salt.
3. Remove the wings from the brine, and pat dry with kitchen paper.
4. Transfer the wings to a very large bowl.
5. Add the BBQ rub, brown sugar, and cornstarch. Toss until well and evenly covered.
6. Smoke the wings for around 2 hours.
7. Remove from the smoker and enjoy.

(TOTAL COOK TIME 3 HOURS 15 MINUTES)

INGREDIENTS FOR 4 SERVINGS
THE MEAT

- 6 whole chicken legs with thighs (2-lbs, 0.9-kgs)

THE MARINADE

- ½ fresh lemon
- 3 garlic cloves, peeled, thinly chopped
- Sea salt – 1-2 tablespoons
- Cumin seeds – 1 teaspoon
- Coriander seeds – 1 teaspoon
- Fennel seeds – 1 teaspoon
- Whole black pepper – 1 teaspoon
- Cayenne pepper – 1 teaspoon
- Paprika – 1 teaspoon
- Plain yogurt – 1 cup

THE SMOKE

- Add cherry flavor wood chips to the wood tray
- Set the Masterbuilt smoker for indirect cooking to 225°F (110°C)
- When the smoker has reached the desired temperature, put an additional batch of wood chips in the wood chip tray
- Fill the water pan to the level recommended in the smoker manual

METHOD

1. Puncture the chicken all over with a metal skewer.
2. Rub the cut side of the lemon all over the chicken followed by the garlic and salt.
3. In a pestle and mortar grind the cumin seeds, coriander seeds, fennel seeds, black pepper, cayenne pepper, paprika and grind to combine entirely.
4. In a bowl, combine the yogurt with the seasoning mix and coat each piece of chicken with the mixture.
5. Transfer the chicken to the fridge and marinate overnight.
6. Remove the chicken from the marinade, shaking off any excess marinade.
7. Arrange the chicken skin side facing downwards on oiled smoker racks and smoke for 3-4 hours, until the chicken registers an internal temperature of 140-160°F (60-70°C). You will need to partially opener the damper after 2 hours of smoking.
8. Serve and enjoy.

SMOKED TURKEY BREAST WITH MISO BUTTER GRAVY

(TOTAL COOK TIME 4 HOURS)

INGREDIENTS FOR 8 SERVINGS

THE MEAT

- 1 boneless, skinless turkey breast (4-lbs, 1.8-kgs)

THE RUB

- 2 tsp kosher salt
- 2 ½ tbsp freshly ground black pepper
- Paprika – 1 teaspoon
- Onion powder – 1 teaspoon
- Garlic powder – 1 teaspoon

THE SAUCE

- Unsalted butter – 1 cup
- Miso – 2 tablespoons
- Soy sauce – 1 teaspoon

THE GRAVY

- Unsalted butter – 2 tablespoons
- All-purpose flour – ¼ cup
- Chicken stock – 2 cups
- Soy sauce – ½ teaspoon
- Miso – ½ teaspoon
- Sea salt – ¼ teaspoon

THE SMOKE

- Add sage wood chips to the wood tray
- Preheat your Masterbuilt smoker to 265°F (130°C)
- When the smoker has reached the desired temperature, put an additional batch of wood chips in the wood chip tray
- Fill the water pan to the level recommended in the smoker manual

METHOD

1. In a small bowl, combine the rub ingredients (salt, black pepper, paprika, onion powder, and garlic powder).
2. Rub the mixture all over the turkey, including its sides.
3. Put the turkey, skin side facing upwards, in the smoker. Smoke until golden, for approximately 2 hours or until the meat registers an internal temperature of 140°F (60°C).
4. Meanwhile, prepare the butter sauce. In a second small bowl, combine the melted butter with the miso and soy sauce.
5. When the turkey reaches the desired temperature, remove it from the smoker and place it between 2 sheets of aluminum foil, dull side of the foil out. Place the meat on the foil toward the edge further away from you. You need to do this to allow enough room to wrap it up entirely later on.
6. Drizzle the miso butter sauce on top of the turkey, and wrap tightly in the foil. Seal the edges to prevent the juices from escaping.
7. Return the turkey to the smoker, skin side facing downwards. It should resemble a boat shape. Continue to cook for approximately 60 minutes, until the meat registers an internal temperature of 160°F (70°C).
8. While in the foil, allow the turkey to rest until the temperature reduces to 140°F (60°C). This will take approximately 25-30 minutes. Open the foil carefully to prevent the juices from spilling out.
9. Slice the turkey while keeping the cooking juices for preparing the gravy.
10. For the gravy: Add the butter to a pan over moderate heat. When melted, add the flour. With a spatula, combine the flour and butter for approximately 2-3 minutes to create a roux.
11. A little at a time, pour in the chicken broth. It is best to do this in ¼ cupfuls and to make sure that the mixture is homogenous before pouring in the next batch of broth.
12. Pour in the meat drippings and stir to combine with the roux. Taste and adjust the seasonings. Add more miso, soy sauce, or salt, as preferred.
13. Turn the heat to moderate to high and while stirring, bring to boil.
14. Once at a boil, reduce the heat to moderate, and while occasionally stirring, cook until the gravy is your preferred thickens.

SPICY SMOKED CHICKEN

(TOTAL COOK TIME 2 HOURS 30 MINUTES)

INGREDIENTS FOR 4 SERVINGS
THE MEAT

- 1 whole chicken, rinsed, giblets removed and patted dry

THE SEASONING

- Garlic powder – 1 teaspoon
- Onion powder – 1 teaspoon
- Cumin – 1 teaspoon
- Paprika – 1 teaspoon
- Allspice – ¼ teaspoon
- Sea salt – ¼ teaspoon
- Freshly ground black pepper – ½ teaspoon
- Ground cloves – ¼ teaspoon

78

THE SMOKE

- Add applewood chips to the wood tray
- Set the Masterbuilt smoker for indirect cooking to 225°F (110°C)
- When the smoker has reached the desired temperature, put an additional batch of wood chips in the wood chip tray
- Fill the water pan to the level recommended in the smoker manual
- Add 2 cups of apple juice to the drippings pan

METHOD

1. To a bowl, add the garlic powder, onion powder, cumin, paprika, allspice, sea salt, black pepper, and ground cloves. Stir well to combine and coat the entire chicken with the mixture.
2. Smoke the chicken for 60 minutes per (1-lbs, 0.45-kgs) in weight.
3. Remove the chicken from the smoker and set aside to rest for several minutes before serving. Enjoy.

(TOTAL COOK TIME 10 HOURS 35 MINUTES)

INGREDIENTS FOR 4 SERVINGS
THE MEAT

- 4 turkey legs

THE BRINE

- Cold water, divided – 5 cups
- Kosher salt – ½ cup
- Runny honey – ¼ cup
- Paprika – 1 tablespoon
- Garlic powder – ½ tablespoons
- Onion powder – ½ tablespoon
- Freshly ground black pepper – ½ tablespoons
- Cayenne pepper – ½ teaspoon
- 4 allspice berries
- Ice cubes – 1 cup

THE SMOKE

- While the smoker is cold, add apple flavor wood chips to the wood tray
- Set the Masterbuilt smoker or indirect cooking to 250°F (120°C)
- When the smoker has reached the desired temperature, put an additional batch of wood chips in the wood chip tray
- Fill the water pan to the level recommended in the smoker manual

METHOD

1. In a large deep-sided pot, combine 3 cups of cold water with salt, honey, paprika, garlic powder, onion powder, black pepper, cayenne, and allspice. Bring to a boil. Pour in the remaining 2 cups of water and the ice cubes. Stir to combine until the ice melts and the mixture reaches room temperature. Add additional ice if needed.
2. Add the turkey legs, two at a time, to jumbo-size ziplock bags.
3. Pour an equal amount of the brine into each bag. Seal the bags and place them in the fridge overnight.
4. The following day, pour the brine away. Rinse the turkey legs until running water, and using kitchen paper towels, pat dry.
5. Place the turkey legs in the preheated smoker, and smoke for 2½-3½ hours until they register an internal temperature of 165°F (75°C).
6. Serve and enjoy.

CITRUS-SEASONED TURKEY BREAST

(TOTAL COOK TIME 28 HOURS 35 MINUTES)

INGREDIENTS FOR 10-12 SERVINGS
THE MEAT

- 1 bone-in turkey breast half, rinsed, patted dry, rib tips trimmed (5-lbs, 2.3-kgs)

THE SEASONING

- 1 lime, lemon, and orange, all quartered and seeded
- ¼ grapefruit, rind on, seeded, and cut into 1-ins (0.4-cms) pieces
- Sea salt – ¼ cup
- Pack sugar, light or dark brown – ¼ cup
- Cracked black peppercorns – 2 tablespoons
- Fennel seeds – 1 tablespoon
- Extra-virgin olive oil, divided – 6 tablespoons
- Water, as needed – ¼ - ½ cup

THE SMOKE

- While the smoker is cold, add your choice of wood chips to the wood tray
- Set the Masterbuilt smoker to 225-250°F (110-120°C)
- When the smoker has reached the desired temperature, put an additional batch of wood chips in the wood chip tray
- Fill the water pan to the level recommended in the smoker manual

METHOD

1. Place the turkey in a jumbo-size ziplock bag.
2. To prepare the citrus seasoning: Add the lime, lemon, and orange quarters to a food processor. Add the grapefruit, sea salt, sugar, black pepper, and fennel seeds and process to a ground coarse paste consistency.
3. Grind in 4 tablespoons of oil and a ¼-½ cup of cold water. Process to a pourable, thick-paste consistency.
4. Pour the mixture into the ziplock bag and over the turkey, gently massaging to ensure an even coating,
5. Seal the bag, put it inside a heavy-duty aluminum foil pan, and place it in the fridge to marinate for 24 hours. You will need to flip the bag repeatedly during the 24 hours to distribute the marinade evenly.
6. Remove the turkey from the bag, and drain on a wire rack set over a rimmed baking sheet. For a rustic look, leave the marinade on the turkey and allow it to dry in the fridge for 2 hours.
7. Place the turkey in the preheated smoker for 60 minutes. After which, begin basting the meat with the remaining oil. You will need to do this every 40-45 minutes. Continue to smoke the turkey until the surface has a smoked-bronzed appearance and the internal temperature of the meat registers 165°F (74°C). This whole process will take around 2-3 hours.
8. When the turkey is cooked, remove it from the smoker and place it on a chopping board. Set aside to rest for 5 minutes before slicing thinly across the grain. Enjoy.

PECAN SMOKED STUFFED TURKEY

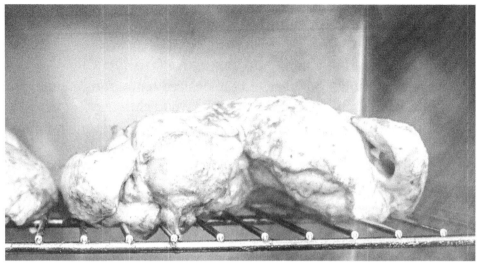

(TOTAL COOK TIME 7 HOURS)

INGREDIENTS FOR 16 SERVINGS
THE MEAT

- 1 whole turkey (12-14-lbs, 3.4-6.4-kgs)

THE INGREDIENTS

- Olive oil – 3 tablespoons
- Unsalted butter, room temperature – 3 tablespoons
- 2 cloves of fresh garlic, peeled and minced
- Dried thyme – 2 tablespoons
- Powdered sage – 1 tablespoon
- Dried oregano – 2 teaspoons
- Seal salt – 2 teaspoons
- Cracked black pepper – 1½ teaspoon
- Dried rosemary – 1 teaspoon
- 1 apple, seeded and quartered
- 1 lemon, cut into quarters, and seeded
- 1 onion, peeled and halved
- Apple cider – ½ cup
- Water, as needed

THE SMOKE

- Add pecan flavor wood chips to the wood tray
- Set the Masterbuilt smoker to 225°F (110°C)
- When the smoker has reached the desired temperature, put an additional batch of wood chips in the wood chip tray
- Fill the water pan with ½ cup of water and ½ cup of apple cider halfway full

METHOD

1. In a bowl, combine the oil with butter, garlic, thyme, sage, oregano, paprika, sea salt, black pepper, and dried rosemary.
2. Rub the turkey's interior cavity with one-third of the mixture. Stuff the cavity with the apple, lemon, and onion quarters and rub the surface with the remaining fat-herb mixture.
3. Place a drip pan on the rack about the water pan in the smoker. Doing this will help to collect any drippings while the bird smokes.
4. Tuck the wing tips tightly beneath the turkey.
5. Put the turkey directly on the smoker's middle rack.
6. Smoke for around 6½ hours. The smoking time is approximately 30-40 minutes per (1-lbs, 0.45-kgs). Check the smoker every 60 minutes, adding apple cider-water if necessary.
7. The turkey is ready when it registers an internal temperature of 165°F (75°C).
8. Remove the bird from the smoker, and set it aside to rest on a chopping board for 20-25 minutes before carving. You may want to tent the bird loosely in aluminum foil to help keep it moist.

STUFFED TURKEY ROLL

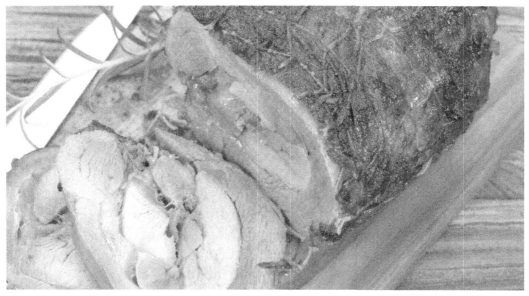

(TOTAL COOK TIME 5 HOURS 20 MINUTES)

INGREDIENTS FOR 6 SERVINGS
THE MEAT

- Boneless turkey breast, butterflied and pounded (2.2-lbs, 1-kgs)

THE INGREDIENTS

- Butter – 2 tablespoons
- Fresh mushrooms, sliced – 2 cups
- 3 green onions, finely chopped
- 1 carrot, chopped small
- 1 stalk of celery, trimmed and finely chopped
- Salt and black pepper
- Poultry seasoning, of choice
- Freshly squeezed lemon juice, as needed
- 2 slices of bread, cut into cubes
- 1 medium tomato, seeded and diced

THE SMOKE

- While the smoker is cold, add maple flavor wood chips to the wood tray
- Set the Masterbuilt smoker to 190-220°F (90-105°C)
- When the smoker has reached the desired temperature, put an additional batch of wood chips in the wood chip tray
- Fill the water pan to the level recommended in the smoker manual

METHOD

1. Heat the butter in a pan and sauté the mushrooms with the onion, carrot, and celery. Add the salt, pepper, and poultry seasoning, followed by 1 tablespoonful of lemon juice.
2. In a bowl, mix the bread cubes with the diced tomato and sautéed veggies from Step 1.
3. Spread the mixture over the butterflied turkey. Rub additional fresh lemon juice over the surface of the skin.
4. Place the turkey roll on a lightly oiled rack in the top half of your smoker.
5. Smoke the meat for 5-6 hours until it registers an internal temperature of 160°F (70°C).
6. Serve and enjoy.

CHAPTER 5
SEAFOOD

CUTS ⹁ CRAB

(TOTAL COOK TIME 6 HOURS 20 MINUTES)

INGREDIENTS FOR 6 SERVINGS
THE FISH

- 6 Ahi tuna steaks (4-ozs, 114-gms) each

THE BRINE

- Kosher salt – 3 tablespoons
- Light brown sugar – 3 tablespoons

THE INGREDIENTS

- Extra-virgin olive oil – ¼ cup
- Lemon pepper seasoning
- Ground garlic – 1 teaspoon
- 12 thin slices of lemon

THE SMOKE

- Add peach wood chips to the wood tray
- Set the Masterbuilt smoker to 190°F (90°C)
- When the smoker has reached the desired temperature, put an additional batch of wood chips in the wood chip tray
- Fill the water pan to the level recommended in the smoker manual

METHOD

1. Season the fish on all sides with salt and sugar. Transfer the seasoned fish to a ziplock bag or sealed container and place in the fridge for 4-8 hours.
2. Remove the tuna from the ziplock bag, and wipe off the majority of the dry brine.
3. Coat both sides of the fish with olive oil, lemon pepper seasoning, and garlic powder.
4. Place the tuna directly on the smoker rack. Add 2 lemon slices on top of each tuna steak. Return to the smoker and smoke for 60 minutes.
5. When 1 hour has elapsed, check the temperature of the fish. The tuna is ready when it registers an internal temperature of 140°F (60°C). If it is not at this temperature, continue to smoke. The total smoking time is 1–1¾ hours.
6. Take the fish out of the smoker and set aside on a chopping board to rest for 2-3 minutes.
7. Serve the fish with lemon wedges.

WHITE WINE MARINATED HALIBUT

(TOTAL COOK TIME 2 HOURS 55 MINUTES)

INGREDIENTS FOR 6 SERVINGS
THE FISH

- Halibut fillets, skin-on (2-lbs, 0.9-kgs)
- Extra-virgin olive oil, to serve
- Caper berries, chopped, to serve– 1 teaspoon
- Wedges of fresh lemon, to serve

THE MARINADE

- Dry white wine – ½ cup
- Extra-virgin olive oil – ¼ cup
- 1 garlic clove, peeled and minced
- Freshly squeezed lemon juice – 2 tablespoons
- Fresh shallots, minced – 1 teaspoon
- Dried tarragon – ½ teaspoon
- Sea salt – ½ teaspoon
- Freshly ground black pepper – ½ teaspoon

THE SMOKE

- While the smoker is cold, add mild flavor chips to the wood tray. Good choices are apple, pecan, or oak
- Set the Masterbuilt smoker with the top vent open to 225°F (110°C)
- After 60 minutes of smoking time, put an additional batch of wood chips in the wood chip tray and replenish the water
- Fill the water pan to the level recommended in the smoker manual. You can add some slices of lemon to the water, but this is optional.

METHOD

1. In a bowl, to prepare the marinade, combine the white wine with the oil, fresh garlic, lemon juice, shallots, tarragon, sea salt, and black pepper. Stir to incorporate.
2. Rinse the halibut until cold running water and pat dry with kitchen paper towels.
3. Add the fish to a large ziplock bag.
4. Pour the marinade over the halibut, seal, and gently massage to evenly coat.
5. Place the bag in a large dish, and transfer to the fridge for 60 minutes.
6. Remove the fish from the fridge and set aside for 15 minutes to come to room temperature.
7. Lay the fish, skin side facing down on a rack, and place in the smoker.
8. Smoke the fish for 1½ -2 hours until it registers an internal temperature of 140°F (60°C).
9. Remove the fish from the smoker and place it on a chopping board. Thinly slice, removing and discarding any skin.
10. Arrange the slices of fish on a serving platter, drizzle with oil, scatter over the caper berries and serve warm with fresh wedges of lemon for squeezing.

SMOKED RED SNAPPER

(TOTAL COOK TIME 2 HOURS 15 MINUTES)

INGREDIENTS FOR 2-3 SERVINGS
THE FISH

- Fresh red snapper filet, skin-on (1.5-lbs, 0.7-kgs)
- Pure maple syrup – 1 tablespoon

THE BRINE

- Sea salt – ¼ cups
- Water – 8 cups
- Brown sugar – 2 tablespoons
- Granulated garlic – 1 tablespoon

THE RUB

- Olive oil- 2 tablespoons
- Brown sugar – 1 tablespoon
- Garlic, peeled and chopped – 1 tablespoon
- Freshly ground black pepper – 1 tablespoon

THE SMOKER

- While the smoker is cold, add alder wood chips to the wood tray Set the Masterbuilt smoker to 225°F (110°C)
- When the smoker has reached the desired temperature, put an additional batch of wood chips in the wood chip tray
- Fill the water pan to the level recommended in the smoker manual

METHOD

1. Brine the fish by dissolving the salt in the water. You may need to add more water or salt. The brine is ready when you able to float an egg in it. Next, add the sugar along with the granulated garlic. Brine the fish for 60 minutes.
2. Rub olive oil all over the fish.
3. In a bowl, combine the brown sugar, garlic, and pepper. Rub the mixture all over the oiled fish.
4. Smoke the fish in the preheated smoker for 60-75 minutes, until it reaches an internal temperature of 145°F (65°C). Timings will depend on the thickness of the fish.
5. Using a pastry brush, brush the top of the fish all over with maple syrup before serving.

GARLIC DILL SALMON

(TOTAL COOK TIME 20 HOURS 15 MINUTES)

INGREDIENTS FOR 12 SERVINGS
THE FISH

- 2 large salmon fillets, pin bones removed

THE BRINE

- Water – 2 cups
- Brown sugar – 1 cup
- Kosher salt - ⅓ cup

THE SEASONING

- Garlic, peeled and minced – 3 tablespoons
- Fresh dill, chopped – 1 tablespoon

THE SMOKE

- While the smoker is cold, add alder wood chips to the wood tray Set the Masterbuilt smoker to 180°F (80°C)
- When the smoker has reached the desired temperature, put an additional batch of wood chips in the wood chip tray
- Fill the water pan to the level recommended in the smoker manual

METHOD

1. In a bowl, thoroughly combine the brine ingredients (water, brown sugar, and kosher salt).
2. Place the fish in the brine, and transfer to the fridge for 16 hours.
3. Remove the salmon from the brine, rinse under cold running water, and, using paper towels, pat dry. Allow the fish to rest uncovered on a rack in the fridge for 2-4 hours until a pellicle forms.
4. Season the fish with garlic and fresh dill.
5. Place the salmon on the rack and smoke the fish in the preheated smoker for 4 hours
6. Remove the fish from the smoker and serve.
7. Enjoy.

TERIYAKI SMOKED TILAPIA

(TOTAL COOK TIME 2 HOURS 10 MINUTES)

INGREDIENTS FOR 4 SERVINGS

THE FISH

- 4 tilapia fillets

THE MARINADE

- Runny honey – ⅔ cup
- Teriyaki sauce, store-bought – 1 tablespoon
- Sriracha sauce – 1 tablespoon

THE SMOKE

- Preheat your Masterbuilt smoker for indirect cooking to 275°F (135°C)
- Add alder, apple, maple, or peach wood chips for this recipe

METHOD

1. First, prepare the marinade by combine the honey with the teriyaki sauce and sriracha until well blended and fully incorporated.
2. Add the fish to a large bowl.
3. Spoon the marinade over the fish and flip over until they are well and evenly coated. Cover the bowl with kitchen wrap and transfer to the refrigerator for approximately 2 hours.
4. Remove the fish from the marinade and place in a smoker.
5. Smoke the tilapia for approximately 2 hours or until they register an internal temperature of 145°F (65°C).
6. Serve and enjoy.

SMOKED OCTOPUS

(TOTAL COOK TIME 17 HOURS 20 MINUTES)

INGREDIENTS FOR 6 SERVINGS
THE SEAFOOD

- 1 whole octopus (4-lb, 1.8-kg)

THE BRINE

- Water – 8 cups
- Sea salt – 4 tablespoons
- Brown sugar – 4 tablespoons
- Red wine vinegar – 2 tablespoons

THE MARINADE

- Olive oil – ¼ cup
- Freshly squeezed lemon juice – ½ cup
- Garlic, peeled and minced – 1 tablespoon
- Dried oregano – 1 tablespoon

THE SMOKE

- While the smoker is cold, add pecan wood chips to the wood tray
- Set the Masterbuilt smoker to 175°F (80°C)

METHOD

1. In a container in a mixture of water, sea salt, brown sugar, and red wine vinegar, brine the octopus overnight.
2. The following day, rinse the octopus and pat dry.
3. Remove the meat from the underside of the octopus. Do this with a knife.
4. In a bowl, combine the marinade, olive oil, lemon juice, garlic, and oregano. Marinade the octopus in the fridge for 4 hours.
5. Cook the octopus in the smoker until it registers an internal temperature of 165°F (75°C). This process will take 5-6 hours. Depending on the size of the octopus.
6. Remove from the smoker, and enjoy.

(TOTAL COOK TIME 2 HOURS 30 MINUTES)

INGREDIENTS FOR 6-8 SERVINGS
THE SEAFOOD

- 24 oysters

THE MARINADE

- Salt – 1 teaspoon
- Worcestershire sauce – ¼ cup
- Sriracha – 1 teaspoon
- Freshly squeezed lemon juice of ½ lemon
- 1 whole garlic clove, peeled
- Lemon zest – 1 teaspoon
- Chives – 1 tablespoon

THE SMOKE

- While the smoker is cold, add your favorite wood chips to the wood tray
- Preheat the Masterbuilt smoker to 200°F (95°C)

METHOD

1. Closely inspect the oysters, looking out for any that are opened or chipped and discard any that are.
2. Holding a cloth in one hand, firmly hold the oyster. With the other hand, use an oyster knife, and insert it carefully into the oyster's hinge. Twist the knife to separate the muscle that holds the shell closed.
3. Remove the oyster from its shells and transfer it to a small container.
4. In a bowl, combine the marinade ingredients (salt, Worcestershire sauce, Sriracha, lemon juice, garlic clove, lemon zest, and chives).
5. Pour the marinade over the oysters, cover the container with a lid and transfer to the fridge for 20 minutes.
6. Remove the oysters from the fridge, return them to the shells, and arrange them on the smoker grates.
7. Smoke the oysters for 2 hours.
8. Serve and enjoy.

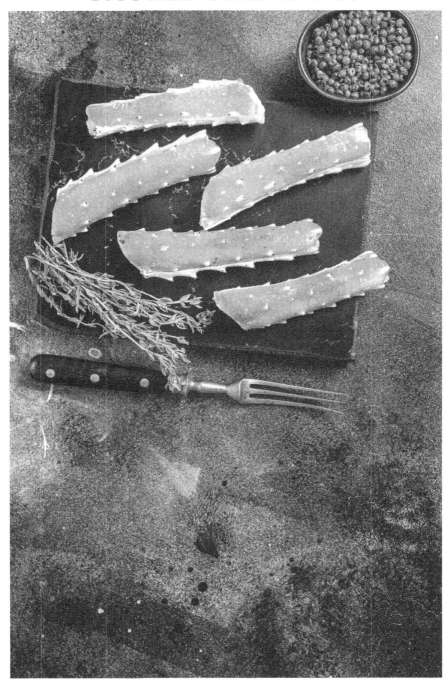

INGREDIENTS FOR 8 SERVINGS
THE SEAFOOD

- Lump crabmeat, picked over (1-lb, 0.45-kg)
- Shrimp, peeled, deveined, and tails removed (4-oz, 113.4-g)

THE INGREDIENTS

- Milk – 1 cup
- Panko breadcrumbs – 1½ cups
- Salt and black pepper, to season
- Onion, peeled and chopped – ½ cup
- 2 garlic cloves, peeled and smashed
- 2 celery ribs, trimmed and chopped
- Unsalted butter – 2 tablespoons
- Heavy cream – ¼ cup
- Hot pepper sauce – 1 teaspoon
- Freshly squeezed lemon juice – 1 teaspoon
- Dijon mustard – 2 teaspoons
- Old Bay seasoning – ¾ teaspoon

THE SMOKE

- Set the Masterbuilt smoker to 250°F (120°C) for indirect cooking
- Add your favorite wood chips to the wood tray

METHOD

1. First, soak the crabmeat in a bowl of milk, and while covered totally, soak it in the fridge for a minimum of 30 minutes.
2. Add the breadcrumbs to a Ziplock bag and crush them using a mallet or rolling pin. Transfer the crushed breadcrumbs to a skillet, and over moderately high heat, toast, while stirring continuously, until golden for around 4 minutes.
3. Transfer the toasted crumbs to a shallow plate and season with ½ teaspoon salt and ½ teaspoon black pepper. Put to one side.
4. Add the onion, garlic, and celery to a food blender and process on pulse 7-8 times.
5. Over moderate heat, preheat a skillet and melt the butter.
6. Then add the pulsed veggies to the skillet and season with ½ teaspoon salt and ½ teaspoon black pepper. Stir the veggies frequently, until tender and most of the moisture evaporated, for around 5 minutes. Transfer the veggies to a big bowl.
7. Press the crabmeat gently against a fine mesh strainer to expel as much milk as possible, but while taking care not to damage any of the crab meat. Discard the milk. Add the shrimp to the blender and pulse 15 times.
8. Next, add the cream and pulse for another 5 times. Scrape down the sides of the blender bowl as necessary.
9. Add the shrimp to the bowl with the cooled veggies, and add the pepper sauce, fresh lemon juice, Dijon mustard, and Old Bay seasoning and stir until combined.
10. Add the crabmeat and fold in until combined.
11. Form the crabmeat mixture into 8 even-size balls.
12. Arrange the crabmeat balls on a parchment-lined baking sheet. Take a spatula and press the balls into patties, around 0.5-in (1.5-cm).
13. Cover the patties with kitchen wrap, and transfer to the fridge for a minimum of 30 minutes.
14. Finally, press each patty into the breadcrumbs until coated and covered. Smoke the crab cakes for 50 minutes or until they reach an internal temperature of 155°F (70°C).
15. Serve and enjoy.

CHAPTER 6
BURGERS AND SAUSAGES

(TOTAL COOK TIME 2 HOURS 30 MINUTES)

INGREDIENTS FOR 4 SERVINGS
THE MEAT

- Fresh ground turkey (2-lbs, 0.9-kgs)

THE INGREDIENTS

- 6 scallions, thinly sliced
- Breadcrumbs – 1 cup
- Barbecue sauce – ½ cup
- Ground oregano – 1 teaspoon
- Garlic powder – 1 teaspoon
- Paprika – 1 teaspoon
- Salt – 1 teaspoon
- Freshly ground black pepper – ½ teaspoon
- Cayenne pepper – ¼ teaspoon

THE SMOKE

- Preheat your Masteerbuilt smoker to 250°F (120°C)
- Apple or pecan wood chips are recommended for this recipe

METHOD

1. In a large-size bowl, combine the ground turkey with the scallions, breadcrumbs, barbecue sauce, ground oregano, garlic powder, paprika, salt, freshly ground black pepper, and cayenne pepper.
2. Using clean hands, knead the mixture to combine and blend entirely.
3. Shape the mixture into 4 evenly-sized pattie shapes and arrange them in a single layer and not touching one another on the smoker racks.
4. Cook, until they register an internal temperature of 165°F (75°C).
5. Serve in a bun with your favorites toppings and sides and enjoy.

(TOTAL COOK TIME 1 HOUR 25 MINUTES)

INGREDIENTS FOR 4 SERVINGS
THE MEAT

- Ground beef chuck (2-lbs, 0.9-kgs)

THE INGREDIENTS

- Sea salt and freshly ground black pepper
- 4 slices American cheese
- Burger buns split, to serve
- Relish, store-bought, to serve, optional

THE SMOKE

- While the smoker is cold, add your favorite wood chips to the wood tray
- Remove the racks
- Set the Masterbuilt smoker to 225°F(110 °C)
- When the smoker has reached the desired temperature, put an additional batch of wood chips in the wood chip tray
- Fill the water pan to the level recommended in the smoker manual

METHOD

1. Using clean hands, form the meat into 4 even-size patties and season all over with salt and black pepper.
2. Return a rack to the smoker.
3. Smoke the patties until they register an internal temperature of 150-160°F (65-70°C) for around 60-90 minutes. When only 15 minutes of smoking time remains, add a slice of American cheese to each burger and continue to smoke until the meat is cooked through and the cheese is melted.
4. Serve the burgers inside the buns, and top with a dollop of your favorite relish.

LAMB BURGERS WITH MINT MAYONNAISE

(TOTAL COOK TIME 45 MINUTES)

INGREDIENTS FOR 2 SERVINGS
THE MEAT

- Minced or ground lamb (2-lbs, 0.9-kgs)

THE MAYONNAISE

- Full-fat mayonnaise – 2 tablespoons
- Fresh mint, chopped – 2 teaspoons
- Mint sauce, prepared – 1 teaspoon

THE BURGERS

- Salt and freshly ground black pepper
- 2 burger buns, split
- Mint mayonnaise, see recipe

THE SMOKE

- Add your favorite wood chips to the wood tray
- Set the Masterbuilt smoker to 225°F (110°C)
- When the smoker has reached the desired temperature, put an additional batch of wood chips in the wood chip tray
- Fill the water pan to the level recommended in the smoker manual

METHOD

1. First, prepare the mint mayonnaise.
2. In a bowl, combine the mayonnaise with the fresh mint and mint sauce. Stir well and transfer to the fridge until needed.
3. Season the lamb generously with salt and pepper.
4. Using clean hands, form the meat into 2 even-size patties.
5. Smoke the patties for 40-45 minutes or until the internal temperature registers 165°F (75°C).
6. Serve the patties inside the buns, top with a spoonful of mint mayonnaise enjoy.

GARDEN HERB TURKEY SAUSAGES

(TOTAL COOK TIME 3 HOURS 35 MINUTES)

INGREDIENTS FOR 8-10 SERVINGS
THE MEAT

- Ground turkey (3-lbs, 1.4-kgs)

THE INGREDIENTS

- ½ onion, peeled and finely diced
- Fresh parsley, finely chopped – 3 tablespoons
- Freshly sage, finely chopped – 3 tablespoons
- Fresh thyme, finely chopped- 2 teaspoons
- Fresh rosemary, finely chopped – 1 teaspoon
- Salt – 3 teaspoons
- Freshly ground black pepper - 1 teaspoon
- Hog casing, as needed

THE SMOKE

- While the smoker is cold, add alder flavor wood chips to the wood tray
- Set the Masterbuilt smoker to 275°F (135°C)
- When the smoker has reached the desired temperature, put an additional batch of wood chips in the wood chip tray
- Fill the water pan to the level recommended in the smoker manual

METHOD

1. In a bowl, combine the ground turkey with the onion, parsley, sage, thyme, rosemary, salt, and black pepper.
2. Soak the hog casing in fresh cold water for half an hour.
3. Flush the hog casing with water.
4. Stuff the casing with the turkey mixture and twist off the links.
5. Hang the sausages in the smoker and smoke until they reach an internal temperature of 165°F (75°C). This process may take up to 3 hours, and you will need to turn the sausages as they cook.
6. Serve and enjoy.

WILD BOAR SAUSAGES

(TOTAL COOK TIME 11 HOURS)

INGREDIENTS FOR 4-6 SERVINGS
THE MEAT

- Ground wild boar (1-lb, 0.5-kgs)

THE INGREDIENTS

- Quick salt tender – 1½ teaspoons
- Kosher salt – 1 tablespoon
- Mustard seeds _ ½ teaspoon
- Black pepper – ½ teaspoon
- Garlic powder– ½ teaspoon

118

THE SMOKE

- Add your favorite wood chips to the wood tray
- Set the Masterbuilt smoker to 225°F (110°C)
- When the smoker has reached the desired temperature, put an additional batch of wood chips in the wood chip tray
- Fill the water pan to the level recommended in the smoker manual

METHOD

1. In a bowl, combine the quick salt tender, kosher salt, mustard seeds, black pepper, and garlic powder and mix lightly. Allow the mixture to rest in the refrigerator for 8 hours.
2. Form the meat into a log-shape and wrap in plastic wrap. Twist the ends of the wrap. Using your finger, smooth out the log. Slowly unwrap, to maintain its even shape.
3. Transfer to the smoker and cook for 3-4 hours.
4. Remove from the smoker and set aside to cool for 1 hour at room temperature.
5. Unwrap, and store in the fridge until needed.

CHAPTER 7
JERKY

BEEF JERKY

(TOTAL COOK TIME 12 HOURS 30 MINUTES)

INGREDIENTS FOR 16 SERVINGS
THE MEAT

- Flank or sirloin steak (5-lbs, 2.3-kgs)

THE MARINADE

- 1 can dark beer
- Soy sauce – ½ cup
- Olive oil – ¼ cup
- Worcestershire sauce – ¼ cup
- Brown sugar - ⅛ cup
- Smoked paprika - 1 tablespoon
- Crushed red pepper – 1 tablespoon
- Hot sauce, of choice – 3 tablespoons
- Garlic powder – 1 tablespoon
- Onion salt – 1 tablespoon
- Sea salt – 1 tablespoon
- Black pepper – 1 tablespoon
- Nonstick cooking spray

THE SMOKE

- While the smoker is cold, add your favorite wood chips to the wood tray
- Set the Masterbuilt smoker to 160-180°F (70-80°C)
- When the smoker has reached the desired temperature, put an additional batch of wood chips in the wood chip tray
- Fill the water pan to the level recommended in the smoker manual

METHOD

1. Begin by marinating the meat. Put the beef in a bowl, and add the beer, soy sauce, olive oil, Worcestershire sauce, brown sugar, paprika, crushed red pepper, hot sauce, garlic powder, onion salt, sea salt, and black pepper. Transfer to the fridge for 4-8 hours.
2. As the smoker begins to reach its desired temperature, strip the meat into small pieces. You can do this using a rolling pin and cutting into strips to an approximate size of 0.25-ins (0.5-cms) thick by 1-ins (2.5-cms) wide.
3. Place the strips of meat on a foil pan sprayed with nonstick cooking spray and place in the smoker. Do not stack the strips.
4. When 2½ hours have elapsed, turn on your dehydrator.
5. Smoke the beef jerky for an additional 30 minutes.
6. Transfer to the dehydrator for 5-6 hours, until pliable.

TUNA JERKY

(TOTAL COOK TIME 7 HOURS 15 MINUTES)

INGREDIENTS FOR 6 SERVINGS
THE FISH

- Tuna fillets, cut into thin strips (2-lbs, 0.9-kgs)

THE BRINE

- Soy sauce – 2 cups
- Runny honey – 3 tablespoons
- Sambal Oelek Indonesian seasoning – 3 tablespoons

THE SMOKE

- While the smoker is cold, add peach wood chips to the tray
- Set the Masterbuilt smoker to 200°F (95°C)
- When the smoker has reached the desired temperature, put an additional batch of wood chips in the wood chip tray
- Fill the water pan to the level recommended in the smoker manual

METHOD

1. Add the soy sauce to a small microwave-safe bowl, and in the microwave, heat for 1-2 minutes.
2. Stir in the honey and Sambal Oelek seasoning until the honey dissolves entirely. Set the brine aside to cool.
3. Add the tuna strips to a glass bowl.
4. Pour the cooled brine over the strip and place in the fridge for 2 hours.
5. Remove the tuna from the fridge, and place on a wire rack. Return to the fridge uncovered to dry out for 1-2 hours.
6. Smoke the tuna strip in the smoker until firm yet pliable, for 3-4 hours.
7. Remove from the smoker, set aside to cool entirely before enjoying.

VENISON JERKY

(TOTAL COOK TIME 18 HOURS 10 MINUTES)

INGREDIENTS FOR 20-24 SERVINGS
THE MEAT

- Venison, cut into 0.5-ins(1.27-cms) slices (6-lbs, 2.72-kgs)

THE MARINADE

- Brown sugar – ½ cup
- Worcestershire sauce – 1/8 cup
- Garlic salt – ½ teaspoon
- Soy sauce – ½ cup
- Dry mustard – ½ teaspoon
- Salt – ¼ cup
- Dash of black pepper
- Water – 3 cups

THE SMOKE

- Preheat your Masterbuilt smoker to 140°F (60°C)
- Mesquite or hickory wood chips are recommended for this recipe

METHOD

1. Cut the slices of venison into strips approximately 0.5-ins (1.5-cms) thick and 5-ins (12-cms) long and 1.5-ins (4-cms) wide.
2. Combine the remaining ingredients (brown sugar, Worcestershire sauce, garlic salt, soy sauce, dry mustard, salt, black pepper, and water) in a bowl, and mix until incorporated.
3. Add the meat and marinade to a ziplock bag, and set aside in the fridge for 6-8 hours.
4. Remove the venison from the bag, and using kitchen towels, pat dry.
5. Dry and smoke for 12-16 hours until the jerky is pliable.
6. Store in the refrigerator.

RABBIT JERKY

(TOTAL COOK TIME 9 HOURS 15 MINUTES)

INGREDIENTS FOR 8-12 SERVINGS
THE MEAT

- Belly flaps from 10 rabbits, fat trimmed, cut into jerky-size slices

THE MARINADE

- Freshly squeezed orange juice – 1 cup
- Soy sauce – 1 cup
- Honey – ½ cup
- Black pepper – 1 tablespoon
- Cayenne pepper – 1 teaspoon
- Fresh ginger, grated – 1 teaspoon
- Pink curing salt – ½ teaspoon

THE SMOKER

- Preheat your Masterbuilt smoker to 160°F (70°C)
- Mesquite or hickory wood chips are recommended for this recipe

METHOD

1. In a glass bowl, combine the orange juice with the soy sauce, honey, black pepper, cayenne pepper, grated ginger, and pink curing salt.
2. Add the rabbit and stir thoroughly to evenly and well coat. Set aside to marinate for 4-8 hours.
3. Dry the rabbit jerky in your dehydrator set at 160°F (70°C), on low in the oven with the door cracked open a few inches, or in your smoker until flexible, but dry. This will take approximately 5-6 hours.

LAMB JERKY

(TOTAL COOK TIME 10 HOURS 15 MINUTES)

INGREDIENTS FOR 12-20 SERVINGS
THE MEAT

- Lamb fillets – (1-lb, 0.45-kgs)

THE INGREDIENTS

- Onion salt – 1 tablespoon
- Liquid smoke – 2 tablespoons
- Soy sauce – 4 tablespoons
- Worcestershire sauce - ⅓ cup
- Hickory seasoning liquid – 1½ teaspoons
- 5-6 drops of Tabasco sauce

THE SMOKE

- Preheat the Masterbuilt smoker to 160-180°F (70-80°C)
- Mesquite or hickory wood chips are recommended for this recipe

METHOD

1. Cut the lamb into 0.25-ins (0.5-cms) strips.
2. Combine the onion salt with the liquid smoke, soy sauce, Worcestershire sauce, hickory seasoning liquid, and Tabasco sauce. Add to a ziplock bag along with the strips of lamb. Seal the bag and transfer to the fridge for 6-24 hours.
3. Remove the meat from the ziplock bag. Smoke the jerky until it is dry, chewy, and pliable. This will take between 4-6 hours.
4. Remove the jerky from the smoker and set aside to rest at room temperature.
5. Enjoy.

CHAPTER 8
GAME MEATS

CUTS OF DUCK

(TOTAL COOK TIME 11 HOURS 35 MINUTES)

INGREDIENTS FOR 8-10 SERVINGS
THE MEAT

- 10-12 small alligator racks (5-lbs, 2.27-kgs)

THE MARINADE

- Buttermilk – 2 cups
- Hot sauce, of choice – ½ tablespoon
- Smoked paprika – 1 tablespoon
- Garlic powder – 2 teaspoons
- Onion powder – 2 teaspoons
- Sea salt – 2 teaspoons

THE INGREDIENTS

- Yellow mustard – ¼ cup
- BBQ dry rub, store-bought, of choice – ½ cup
- Apple juice – ½ cup
- BBQ sauce, of choice – 2 cups

THE SMOKE

- Preheat your Masterbuilt smoker to 250°F (120°C)
- Hickory wood chips are recommended for this recipe

METHOD

1. First, prepare the marinade: In a bowl, while whisking, combine the buttermilk with the hot sauce, paprika, garlic powder, onion powder, and salt.
2. Evenly divide the ribs between two ziplock bags and cover with an equal amount of marinade. Seal and place in the fridge overnight.
3. The following day, remove the ribs from the marinade, rinse until cold water and using kitchen paper towels, pat dry.
4. Coat the ribs all over with yellow mustard.
5. Add an even layer of the dry rub seasoning over the mustard.
6. Transfer the ribs to the smoker, cover, and smoke for 90 minutes.
7. Take the ribs out of the smoker, and arrange 3-4 racks on double layer of foil. Fold the foil up on the sides and sprinkle 2 tablespoons of apple juice over the ribs. Securely wrap the foil to completely seal the ribs and juice and return to the smoker.
8. Cover and cook for an additional 1½ -2 hours. The ribs are cooked when they easily bend.
9. Remove from the smoker and carefully unwrap the foil to allow the steam to escape easily.
10. Brush the ribs on both sides with the BBQ sauce and return to the smoker for an additional 10 minutes, until tacky and set.
11. Take the ribs off the smoker, set aside for 4-5 minutes before slicing.

(TOTAL COOK TIME 7 DAYS 2 HOURS 30 MINUTES)

INGREDIENTS FOR 10-12 SERVINGS
THE MEAT

- 1 elk roast (5-lb, 2-kg)

THE CURE

- Kosher salt – ½ teaspoon
- Sugar – ½ teaspoon

THE SMOKE

- Preheat the smoker to 200°F (95°C)
- Choose your favorite wood chips

METHOD

1. Place the meat on a baking sheet.
2. For the cure. In a small bowl, combine the kosher salt with the sugar.
3. Rub the cure all over the meat.
4. Transfer the meat and any loose cure into a ziplock bag. Transfer to the fridge for 7-10 days. You will need to turn the elk roast over once a day.
5. Rinse the meat and pat dry.
6. Smoke the meat for 2-5 hours, or until it reaches an internal temperature of 130°F (55°C).
7. Allow to rest for 10 minutes before slicing.
8. Serve and enjoy.

(TOTAL COOK TIME 2 ½ DAYS)

INGREDIENTS FOR 4 SERVINGS
THE MEAT

- Bison brisket (3-lb, 1.5-kg)

THE INGREDIENTS

- Kosher salt and black pepper, as needed, to season
- Dark red ale, any brand, quantity as needed
- BBQ sauce, any brand, quantity as needed
- Chicken stock, quantity as needed
- Olive oil, as needed

THE SMOKE

- Set the Masterbuilt smoker to 200°F (95°C) for indirect cooking

METHOD

1. Generously season the meat on all sides with salt and black pepper. Transfer to the fridge for 48 hours before smoking.
2. Once you are ready to begin smoking, lay the meat on the smoker's rack and smoke for 2 hours.
3. When 2 hours have elapsed, the meat should have an internal temperature of around 120°F (50°C). Then, coat the meat all over with oil. Smoke for another 30 minutes.
4. Drizzle ale and BBQ sauce over the meat, followed by chicken stock.
5. With pink butcher paper, wrap the bison brisket.
6. Place the meat in a foil tray and return to the smoker. You will need to check every 60 minutes to ensure enough liquid exists to keep the meat moist.
7. After 4½ hours, increase the smoker's temperature to 240°F (115°C). Continue checking on the meat's smoking process every 60 minutes, adding more liquid as needed.
8. When 12-14 hours have elapsed, and the meat has reached an internal temperature of around 200°F (95°C), remove from the smoker. Cover the tray and meat wrapped tightly with foil and allow to cool for 60 minutes before slicing.
9. Enjoy

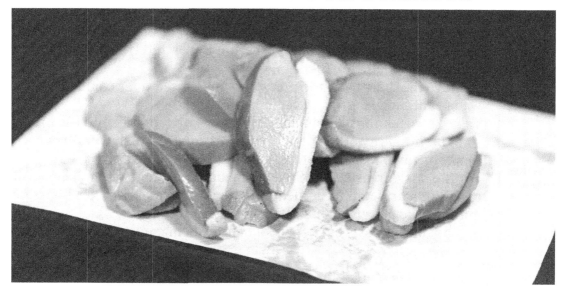

(TOTAL COOK TIME 15 HOURS 10 MINUTES)

INGREDIENTS FOR 8 SERVINGS
THE MEAT

- 2 boneless, skin-on duck breast halves
- Kosher salt – 2 tablespoons
- Cracked black pepper – 2 tablespoons

THE INGREDIENTS

- Maple syrup, divided – 3 tablespoons + 2 teaspoons

THE SMOKE

- While the smoker is cold, add maple wood chips to the wood tray
- Set the Masterbuilt smoker to 225°F (110°C)
- When the smoker has reached the desired temperature, put an additional batch of wood chips in the wood chip tray
- Fill the water pan to the level recommended in the smoker manual

METHOD

1. First, season the duck breasts all over with salt and black pepper. Place the seasoned breasts in a shallow bowl or dish and coat them with three tablespoons of maple syrup. Cover and transfer to the fridge to marinate for 12-24 hours.
2. Remove the duck from the marinade and rinse under cold running water. Pat the meat dry with kitchen paper towels.
3. Take a sharp knife and cut shallow cross-hatch marks into the breast skin, taking care not to cut all the way through. Brush with the remaining two teaspoons of maple syrup.
4. Put the duck breasts, skin side facing upwards on your smoker's grill rack. Put a drip pan underneath the rack and smoke for 3-4 hours or until the meat registers an internal heat of 160°F (70°C).
5. Set the duck breasts aside to cool before slicing and serving.

SMOKED BBQ WILD RABBIT

(TOTAL COOK TIME 3 HOURS 30 MINUTES)

INGREDIENTS FOR 2-3 SERVINGS
THE MEAT

- 1 cottontail rabbit, skinned and gutted

THE BRINE

- Kosher salt – 2 tablespoons
- White vinegar – ½ cup
- Water

THE RUB

- Garlic powder – 1 tablespoon
- Cayenne pepper – 1 tablespoon
- Salt – 1 tablespoon
- Freshly ground black pepper – 1 tablespoon
- 1 store-bought bottle of BBQ sauce

THE SMOKE

- Preheat the Materbuilt smoker to 200°F (93°C)
- Hickory wood chips are a good choice for this recipe

METHOD

1. Add the rabbit to a shallow dish.
2. For the brine: Dissolve the salt in the vinegar and pour it over the rabbit. Add sufficient water to cover and allow the rabbit to brine for a minimum of 60 minutes.
3. Take the rabbit out of the brine and pat dry.
4. Whisk equal parts of garlic powder, cayenne pepper, salt, and pepper in a bowl.
5. Liberally season the rabbit with the rub.
6. Add the rabbit to the smoker and smoke for 15 minutes. Mop the rabbit with the BBQ sauce, repeating every 15 minutes.
7. When 2 hours have elapsed, take the rabbit out of the smoker, mop with BBQ sauce, and serve.

SMOKED PULLED BOAR ON MAC N' CHEESE

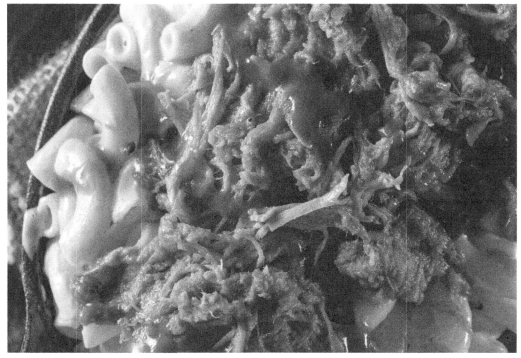

(TOTAL COOK TIME 6 HOURS 35 MINUTES)

INGREDIENTS FOR 1-2 SERVINGS
THE MEAT

- Wild boar shoulder (5-lbs, 2.3-kgs)

THE BRINE

- Water (1-gal, 4-lts)
- Sugar – 1 cup
- Kosher salt – 1 cup
- Black peppercorns – 1 tablespoon
- 1 bunch of fresh thyme, washed
- 1 head of garlic, peeled, halved
- 1 bunch of fresh parsley, washed

THE RUB

- Smoked paprika – 1 cup
- Brown sugar – ¼ cup
- Celery salt – ½ cup
- Granulated garlic – 3 tablespoon
- Cayenne pepper – 1 teaspoon
- Freshly ground black pepper – 1 teaspoon
- Salt – ½ teaspoon

THE SAUCE

- Ketchup – 1 cup
- Apple cider vinegar – 1 cup
- 4 chipotle peppers in adobo sauce
- Brown sugar – 3 tablespoons
- Sea salt – ½ teaspoon

THE MAC N' CHEESE

- Butter – 3 tablespoons
- All-purpose flour – ¼ cup
- Salt – ½ teaspoon
- Black pepper – ¼ teaspoon
- Whole milk – 2 ½ cups
- Macaroni noodles (8-ozs, 227-gms)
- Cheddar cheese, grated – 3 cups
- Chives, to garnish

THE SMOKE

- Preheat your Masterbuilt smoker to 250-300°F (120-150°C)
- Pecan or mesquite wood chips are recommended for this recipe

METHOD

1. For the brine: In a large stockpot, bring the water to simmer. Add the sugar along with the kosher salt, and bring to boil while stirring to incorporate and entirely melt the sugar and salt. Remove the pot from the heat.
2. Next, add the peppercorns followed by the thyme, garlic, and parsley. Allow the water to come to room temperature, before transferring to the fridge to chill.
3. For the rub, in a bowl combine all the ingredients (smoked paprika, brown sugar, celery salt, granulated garlic, cayenne pepper, black pepper, and salt).
4. For the sauce: Combine all the ingredients (ketchup, apple cider vinegar, chipotle pepper, brown sugar, and sea salt) in a food processor and process until silky smooth. Simmer in a pan over low heat for 10 minutes.
5. Season the meat with the spice rub and place it in the smoker. Smoke until it reaches an internal temperature of 180°F (80°C). This will take between 3-4 hours.
6. Shred the meat and toss evenly in the barbecue sauce.
7. For the Mac n' Cheese: Over moderate heat, in a pan, add the butter to melt.
8. Once melted, add the flour followed by the salt and black pepper and whisk for 2-3 minutes.
9. Continue whisking and gradually in a steady stream, pour in the milk, while continuing to stir for 10-12 minutes, until the sauce thickens.
10. Cook the pasta in a pan of boiling water until al dente. Drain and rinse in cold water.
11. Combine the drained pasta with the cheese sauce.
12. Top the Mac n' Cheese with the cooked meat, and garnish with chopped chives.

CHAPTER 9
VEGGIES

(TOTAL COOK TIME 3 HOURS 10 MINUTES)

INGREDIENTS FOR 8 SERVINGS
THE VEGETABLES

- 8   potatoes, scrubbed with eyes removed

THE INGREDIENTS

- Extra-virgin olive oil
- Kosher salt
- Butter, to serve
- Freshly ground black pepper

THE SMOKE

- Preheat your electric smoker to 250°F (120°C)
- Add cherry wood chips
- Pour in sufficient water to fill water bowl to halfway full

METHOD

1. First, with a metal fork, pierce the unpeeled potatoes several times. Brush with olive oil and season with kosher salt.
2. Arrange the potatoes on the top rack and smoke for between 2-3 hours, until fork tender.
3. Serve the potatoes with butter and season with salt and freshly ground black pepper.
4. Enjoy!

OAK SMOKED MUSHROOMS

(TOTAL COOK TIME 2 HOURS 10 MINUTES)

INGREDIENTS FOR 4-6 SERVINGS
THE VEGETABLES

- 10-12 large Portobello mushrooms, stemmed, and dry wiped

THE INGREDIENTS

- Extra-virgin olive oil, as needed
- Sea salt and freshly ground black pepper to season
- Herbs de Provence, to season

THE SMOKE

- While the smoker is cold, add oak wood chips to the wood tray
- Set the Masterbuilt smoker to 200°F (90°C)
- When the smoker has reached the desired temperature, put an additional batch of wood chips in the wood chip tray
- Fill the water pan to the level recommended in the smoker manual; around halfway is good

METHOD

1. Rub the prepared mushrooms with olive oil all over and season with salt and freshly ground black pepper.
2. Scatter the Herbs de Provence seasoning inside the bowl of the mushroom caps.
3. Put the mushrooms, cap side facing downward, directly on your smoker's rack, and smoke for around 2 hours. You will need to refill the water bowl and wood chip tray every 40-60 minutes.
4. Remove the mushrooms carefully from the rack, taking care not to spill any of the caps' liquid.
5. Serve and enjoy.

SMOKED GREEN CABBAGE

(TOTAL COOK TIME 2 HOURS 10 MINUTES)

INGREDIENTS FOR 4 SERVINGS
THE VEGETABLES

- 1 small head green cabbage, 2 outer leaves removed, rinsed well, and patted dry

THE INGREDIENTS

- Balsamic vinegar
- Sea salt – ½ teaspoon

- Freshly ground black pepper – ½ teaspoon
- Butter – 2 tablespoons
- Extra-virgin olive oil, as needed
- Water and naturally sweetened pure apple juice – 1 tablespoon

THE SMOKE

- Add apple flavor wood chips to the wood tray
- Set the Masterbuilt smoker to 225°F (110°C)
- When the smoker has reached the desired temperature, put an additional batch of wood chips in the wood chip tray
- Fill the water pan halfway with a mixture of half water and half pure apple juice

METHOD

1. Take a sharp knife, and remove the cabbage's core to create a cylindrical cavity that is approximately 3-ins (7-cms) deep and 1-25-ins (3-cms) wide. Do not cut through to the head.
2. Fill the cabbage cavity with vinegar, and season with salt, black pepper, and butter.
3. Rub the outer head of the cabbage with oil and season once more with salt and black pepper.
4. Using aluminum foil, create a bowl shape. Set the cabbage in the foil bowl. The bowl should be large enough to allow you to close the foil around the cabbage head later. Rest the cabbage in the aluminum foil bowl with the cut end facing upwards.
5. Put the bowl and cabbage on the smoker rack and smoke for 90 minutes. You will need to add more wood chips and replenish the water-juice mixture every 45-60 minutes.
6. Remove the cabbage from the smoker, and close the foil entirely around its heat. Return to the smoker and smoke for an additional 30 minutes.
7. Slice into wedges and serve.

SMOKED GREEN BEANS WITH FLAKED ALMONDS

(TOTAL COOK TIME 2 HOURS 25 MINUTES)

INGREDIENTS FOR 4-6 SERVINGS
THE VEGETABLES

- Fresh green beans, ends trimmed (1-lb, 0.45-kgs)

THE INGREDIENTS

- Italian dressing, store-bought, of choice, as needed
- Freshly squeezed juice of ½ lemon
- Water, as needed
- Flaked almonds, to garnish, optional

THE SMOKE

- Preheat your electric smoker to 200-225°F (95-110°C)
- Oak wood chips are suitable for this recipe
- Pour in sufficient water to half fill the bowl

METHOD

1. First, prepare the green beans. Wash and trim the beans and soak in a bowl filled with cold water for 1-2 hours.
2. Remove the beans from the water and pat dry.
3. Add the beans in a single layer to a rectangular shape foil pan.
4. Lightly coat the beans with the Italian dressing.
5. Put the foil tray on the smoker's upper shelf and cook for around 60 minutes.
6. Remove the beans from the heat and drizzle with fresh lemon juice.
7. Close the foil around the hot green beans, or cover with aluminum foil and set aside for 15 minutes, to rest.
8. When you are ready to serve garnish with flaked almonds.

SMOKED JALAPENOS

(TOTAL COOK TIME 4 HOURS 5 MINUTES)

INGREDIENTS FOR 15-20 SERVINGS
THE INGREDIENTS

- Large, ripe jalapenos (2-lb, 0.9-kg)

THE SMOKE

- Set the Masterbuilt smoker to 250°F (120°C)
- Use pecan or apple wood chips for this recipe

METHOD

1. Place the jalapenos along with their stems, seeds and membranes rack in a single layer, a little apart on a smoker rack or tray. Close the lid and smoke the jalapenos. Place the peppers on the hotspot, as this will avoid you having to move them around.
2. Smoke for 4 hours, checking their progress every 60 minutes. They are ready when they are blackened and dark and appear leather-like.
3. Remove from the smoker and enjoy.

CHAPTER 10
SAUCES

LEMON BUTTER SAUCE

(TOTAL TIME 5 MINUTES)

INGREDIENTS FOR ⅓ CUP

THE INGREDIENTS

- Unsalted butter, chopped into pieces – ¼ cup
- 1 garlic clove, peeled and grated
- Sea salt – ¼ teaspoon
- Freshly squeezed lemon juice – 2 tablespoons
- Freshly ground black pepper, to season
- Fresh parsley, chopped, to garnish
- A pinch of red pepper flakes, to serve, optional

METHOD

1. Over low heat, and in a small pan, melt the butter.
2. Add the garlic and salt to the pan and cook for 60 seconds.
3. Take the pan off the heat, and add the fresh lemon juice. Season with pepper and sprinkle over the chopped parsley and red pepper flakes.
4. Serve the sauce with fish, over pasta or rice.

(TOTAL TIME 10 MINUTES)

INGREDIENTS FOR 18 SERVINGS
THE INGREDIENTS

- Dijon mustard – 2 cups
- Fresh parsley, minced – 1 cup
- Dried orange peel – ½ cup
- Rosemary leaves, crushed – ½ cup
- Black pepper – ¼ cup
- Salt – 1 tablespoon

METHOD

1. Combine the mustard, parsley, orange peel, rosemary leaves, black pepper, and salt.
2. Use as directed.

(TOTAL TIME 25 MINUTES)

INGREDIENTS FOR 3½ CUPS
THE INGREDIENTS

- Fresh sweet cherries, stemmed and pitted – 2 cups
- Water, divided - ⅔ cup + 1 tablespoon
- Brown sugar – ½ cup
- Tomato paste – 1 tablespoon
- Balsamic vinegar – 3 tablespoons
- Garlic, peeled and minced – 1 teaspoon
- Salt
- A pinch of red chili flakes
- Cornstarch – 1 tablespoon

METHOD

1. Combine the cherries, ⅔ cup water, sugar, tomato paste, balsamic vinegar, garlic, salt, and red pepper flakes in a pot. Over moderate to high heat, bring to a boil. Turn the heat down to moderate heat and simmer until the fruit is softened and the sauce is reduced slightly. This step will take around 10 minutes.
2. Using an immersion blender, puree the cherries. Strain the puree through a fine-mesh strainer and remove and discard the skins.
3. Return the puree to the pot and bring to a simmer over moderate heat.
4. In a small bowl, combine the cornstarch with one tablespoon of water. Whisk the slurry a little at a time into the sauce until you achieve your preferred consistency.
5. Allow the sauce to cool and store in a suitable container in the fridge for no more than 3 weeks. Serve with chicken or pork.

PINEAPPLE BROWN SUGAR BBQ SAUCE

(TOTAL COOK TIME 8 HOURS 30 MINUTES)

INGREDIENTS FOR 2 CUPS
THE INGREDIENTS

- Pineapple juice – 1 cup
- Packed brown sugar – ¾ cup
- Garlic, peeled and chopped – ½ teaspoon
- Worcestershire sauce – 2 tablespoons
- Ketchup – ¾ cup
- Pinch of red pepper flakes
- Onion powder – ½ teaspoon
- Pinch of salt
- Cornstarch – 1-2 tablespoons
- Water – 1-2 tablespoons

METHOD

1. In a pan, combine the pineapple juice with the brown sugar, garlic, Worcestershire sauce, ketchup, red pepper flakes, onion powder, and salt.
2. Bring to boil before reducing to moderate to low heat and simmer for 12-15 minutes, or until the flavors blend.
3. Mix in an equal amount of cornstarch and water. Gradually add the slurry to the sauce, and while stirring, simmer until you achieve your preferred consistency.
4. Serve with meat or poultry.

SPICY PINK GRAPEFRUIT AND HERB MARINADE FOR FISH

(TOTAL TIME 10 MINUTES)

INGREDIENTS FOR 4 SERVINGS
THE INGREDIENTS

- 1 large pink grapefruit
- Olive oil – ¼ cup
- Honey – 2 tablespoons
- Soy sauce – 3 tablespoons
- Fresh basil, chopped – 1 tablespoon
- Fresh rosemary, chopped – 1 tablespoon
- Red pepper flakes, crushed - ⅛ teaspoon
- 2 garlic cloves, peeled and chopped

166

METHOD

1. Use a zester to grate 1 teaspoon of zest from the grapefruit and add to a bowl. Cut the grapefruit in half and squeeze the juice from the fruit into the bowl with the zest.
2. To the same bowl, add the oil, honey, soy sauce, basil, rosemary, red pepper flakes, and garlic. Stir to combine and pour over your choice of fish.
3. For best results, allow the marinade to soak for at least an hour.

CAROLINA MOPPING SAUCE

(TOTAL TIME 10 MINUTES)

INGREDIENTS FOR 16 SERVINGS
THE INGREDIENTS

- Distilled white vinegar – 1 cup
- Cider vinegar – 1 cup
- Red pepper flakes – 1 tablespoon
- Hot sauce – 1 tablespoon
- Garlic powder – 1 teaspoon
- Onion powder – 1 teaspoon
- Packed brown sugar – 2 tablespoons
- Dry mustard – 1 teaspoon
- Salt – ½ teaspoon
- Ground black pepper – ¼ teaspoon

METHOD

1. Combine the white vinegar, cider vinegar, red pepper flakes, hot sauce, garlic powder, onion powder, brown sugar, dry mustard, salt, and black pepper in a bowl.
2. Transfer to an airtight resealable container and store in the fridge for up to 28 days.
3. Use as directed.

MOROCCAN-STYLE MARINADE

(TOTAL TIME 5 MINUTES)

INGREDIENTS FOR ⅗ CUP
THE INGREDIENTS

- 2 garlic cloves, peeled
- Rose harissa – 1 tablespoon
- Ground cumin – 1 teaspoon
- Ground coriander – 1 teaspoon
- Freshly squeezed lemon juice – 1 tablespoon
- Olive oil – 3 tablespoons
- Runny honey – 1 teaspoon
- Flaked sea salt – ½ teaspoon
- Coarsely ground black pepper to season

METHOD

1. Flatten the garlic cloves and place in a bowl with the end of a rolling pin.
2. Add the rose harissa, cumin, coriander, fresh lemon juice, olive oil, honey, sea salt, and a liberal amount of black pepper to the bowl. Stir well to combine.
3. Use as needed.

SESAME SPICE RUB

(TOTAL TIME 8 MINUTES)

INGREDIENTS FOR ½ CUP

THE INGREDIENTS

- Spanish paprika – ¼ cup
- Ground cumin – 1½ teaspoons
- Sesame seeds – 2 teaspoons
- Dried oregano – 2 teaspoons
- Ground pepper – ½ teaspoon

METHOD

1. In a small resealable airtight container, combine the Spanish paprika, cumin, sesame seeds, oregano, and ground pepper. Cover with a lid, and shake well to incorporate.
2. Store the spice rub at room temperature for up to 12 weeks.
3. Use as directed.

DILL PICKLE JUICE MOP FOR POULTRY AND PORK

(TOTAL TIME 35 MINUTES)

INGREDIENTS FOR 2½-3 CUPS
THE INGREDIENTS

- Butter – ½ cup
- 1 medium onion, peeled and grated
- Dill pickle juice – 1 cup
- Cider vinegar – ¼ cup
- Sugar – ½ cup
- 2 lemons, thinly sliced
- Crushed red pepper – 2 teaspoons
- Cayenne pepper – 2 teaspoons
- Worcestershire sauce – 2 tablespoons
- Salt – ¼ teaspoon
- Black pepper – ¼ teaspoon

METHOD

1. In a pan over moderate heat, melt the butter.
2. Then add the onion and cook for 8-10 minutes, until softened.
3. Stir in the pickle juice, cider vinegar, sugar, lemon slices, crushed red pepper, cayenne pepper, Worcestershire sauce, salt, and black pepper. Simmer for 20 minutes.
4. Use the mop sauce as directed.
5. Serve any leftover sauce warm and on the side.

(TOTAL TIME 15 MINUTES)

INGREDIENTS FOR ⅛ CUP
THE INGREDIENTS

- Honey – 1 tablespoon
- Dijon mustard – 1 tablespoon
- Soy sauce – 1 tablespoon
- 1 garlic clove, peeled and minced

METHOD

1. Combine the honey, Dijon mustard, soy sauce, and garlic in a small bowl. Stir to incorporate.
2. Use the baste for pork chops while basting frequently.
3. This recipe is enough for 4 pork chops.

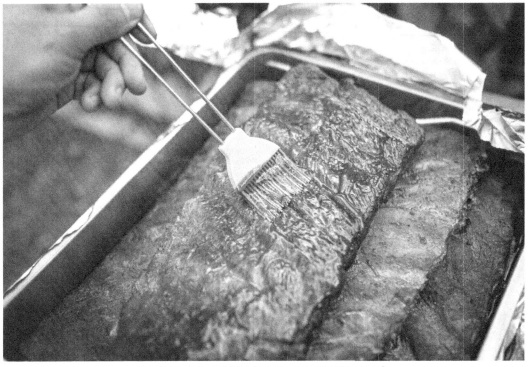

(TOTAL TIME 10 MINUTES)

INGREDIENTS FOR 2 SERVINGS
THE INGREDIENTS

- Apple cider vinegar – 2 cups
- Water – 1 cup
- Memphis rub – ¼ cup
- BBQ sauce, any brand – ¼ cup

METHOD

1. Combine the apple cider vinegar, water, rub, and BBQ sauce in a bowl.
2. Stir well to incorporate and use as directed.

(TOTAL TIME 10 MINUTES)

INGREDIENTS FOR ½ CUP
THE INGREDIENTS

- Butter, cubed – ½ cup
- Dried rosemary, crushed – ½ teaspoon
- Dried tarragon – ½ teaspoon
- Salt – ¾ teaspoon
- Fresh lemon juice – 1 tablespoon

METHOD

1. Combine the butter, rosemary, tarragon, salt, and lemon juice in a small saucepan. Over low heat, cook until the butter melts. Set aside to cool.
2. Use as directed.

CHAPTER 11
SMOKING
MEAT BASICS

In short, electric smokers have paved the way for every American to enjoy the delight of smoked meat from the comfort of their home. These electric smokers are, therefore, often advertised with the tagline "Set it and Forget It," which quickly gives an idea of the core functionality of the appliance. Electric smokers quickly provide the option to smoke meats through an easy-to-use and accessible interface. Since modern electric smokers are packed with intelligent software, the smoker monitors the temperature throughout the smoking process without requiring human involvement. All you have to do is set it up and allow the smoker to do its magic!

BASIC FEATURES

Smokers from different brands are bound to have some tricks, some features almost staple to every electric smoker. Having a good knowledge of these base features will give you a clear idea of what you are going into!

CONSIDERABLY SPACIOUS: Most Electric Smokers are usually very spacious to allow you to smoke meat for a large group of people. Generally speaking, the size of the Electric Smoker ranges from 527 square inches to 730 square inches.

LIGHT WEIGHT: Regular charcoal smokers are bulky and even tough to move! Modern Electric Smokers tend to be highly soft in weight, which makes them easier to move and very mobile. An average Electric Smoker usually weighs somewhere around 40-60 pounds. The inner walls of the smokers are made of stainless steel, which makes them lightweight and durable.

CONSTRUCTION: Normally, most Electric Smokers, are built with durability kept in mind. The design of an Electric Smoker and the ergonomics are often designed with very high-quality imported materials that give it a very long-lasting and safe build. These appliances are 100% safe for both you and your family.

CHROME COATED RACKS: Bigger-sized smokers are often divided into 2-4 compartments that are fully plated with a high-quality chrome. These racks are very easy to remove and can be used to keep large pieces of meat without making a mess. Even the most basic electric smokers tend to have at least four chrome-coated racks.

EASILY CLEANABLE: As Electric Smokers are getting increasingly advanced, they are also becoming more accessible and easy to use. The Stainless Steel walls mean you can easily smoke your meat and veggies and easily clean the smoker afterward.

SAFE TO USE: Electric Smokers are generally built with much grace and don't pose any harm. However, a degree of caution is always to be kept. As long as you follow the guidelines and maintain proper safety procedures, there's no risk of accidental burns or electric shocks from a smoker.

THE BASIC STEPS

Now, the good news for all of your smoke enthusiasts is that using an Electric Smoker isn't rocket science! It means anyone can use it, following some basic and simple guidelines. So it would be best to go through this section before smoking your meat. After all, you don't want your expensive cut to be ruined just because of some silly mishap, right?

Just follow the basics, and you will be fine!
- The first step is to make sure that you always wear safety gloves
- Take out the chips tray and add your wood chips (before smoking begins)
- However, once the smoking has started, you can easily use the side chip tray to add your chips
- The additional chips are required to infuse the meat with a more smoky flavor
- Once the chip bay is ready, load up your marinated meat onto the grill directly
- The stainless steel rack is made for direct smoking; however, if you wish, you can use a stainless steel container to avoid drippings
- Once the meat is in place, lock the door of the chamber
- Turn your smoker "On" using the specified button and adjust the temperature
- Wait until it is done!

Remember that the abovementioned steps are merely basic; different recipes might require additional steps. Either way, they won't be much complicated as, well!

YOUR FIRST ELECTRIC SMOKER

Buying an Electric Smoker is by no means an easy investment. They are generally quite expensive and require a lot of effort and dedication to get one. Due to the sheer variety of Electric Smokers though, it sometimes gets really difficult for an individual to find and purchase the one that is best for their needs. Especially if that individual is a complete beginner in this field. I wanted to make sure that you don't fall victim to such an event, as the feeling of making an unsatisfactory purchase is all but joyful! Therefore, in the following section, I have broken down the key elements that you should keep an eye out for while making your first Electric Smoker purchase. After this section, you will also find a list of the Top 10 Electric Smoker (At the time writing) that your money can buy! That being said, here are the factors to consider.

PRICE: This is perhaps the most decisive part of your purchase. Always make sure to do a lot of research in order to find the best one that falls within your budget (the provided list will help you). However, you should keep in mind that going for the cheapest one might not be a good idea!

As much tempting as they might sound, the quality of the build materials and the finished meal won't be up to mark.

Asides from that, things to keep in mind include

- The reviews
- Safety ratings
- Warranty of the device

CAPACITY: Electric smokers come in different sizes, and you are bound to find one that will suit your need. Before purchasing your Electric Smoker, the things that you should consider in terms of capacity include the following:

- Decide the place where you are going to keep your smoker and hot it will be stored
- Assess the size of your family and how much meat you are going to cook in each batch

Depending on your smoking experience, you will need a larger-capacity smoker if you tend to throw a lot of events! But if it's for personal use, a reasonably small one will do.

BRAND: At the time of writing, Bradley and Masterbuilt were at the forefront of the Electric Smoker market. However, some other brands include Smoke Hollow, Esinkin, and Char-Broil.

A good idea is to not rely on a brand too much but rather look at the specific models and assess the one that suits your needs (depending on the features of the smoker)

DURABILITY: Always keep the device's durability (even if it costs an extra dollar)!

As mentioned earlier, a Smoker is an expensive investment, and you want to buy one that will last you for years.

Two of the most significant issues when it comes to durability that you should keep in mind are

- The quality of the thermostat
- Quality of the seal

If your smoker is properly sealed up, it will require less heat to control and prevent the smoke from escaping and will allow the veggies and meat to be penetrated by the smoke evenly, giving more delicious meals.

SAFE AND ACCESSIBILITY: Even though you are an experienced smoker or a beginner, always read through every single functionality of the smoker that you are considering. Read the provided manufacturer's guide to better educate yourself on the smoker and assess how safe and accessible the smoker might be for you. (According to your experience level)

GENERAL INFORMATION

BARBECUING AND SMOKING MEAT

You might not believe it, but there are still people who think that the process of Barbequing and Smoking are the same! So, this is something you should know about before diving deeper. So, whenever you use a traditional

BBQ grill, you always put your meat directly on top of the heat source for a brief amount of time which eventually cooks up the meal. Smoking, on the other hand, will require you to combine the heat from your grill as well as the smoke to infuse a delicious smoky texture and flavor into your meat. As a result, smoking usually takes much longer than traditional barbecuing. In most cases, it takes a minimum of 2 hours and a temperature of 100 -120 degrees for the smoke to be properly infused into the meat. Keep in mind that the time and temperature will depend on the type of meat you are using, which is why it is suggested to keep a meat thermometer handy to ensure that your meat is doing fine. Also, remember that this barbecuing method is also known as "Low and slow" smoking. With that cleared up, you should be aware that there are two different ways smoking is done.

Depending on the type of grill that you are using, you can get the option to go for a Hot Smoking Method or a Cold Smoking One. However, the primary fact about these three different cooking techniques which you should keep in mind are as follows:

- **HOT SMOKING**: In this technique, the food will use both the heat on your grill and the smoke to prepare your food. This method is most suitable for chicken, lamb, brisket, etc.

- **COLD SMOKING:** In this method, you are going to smoke your meat at a very low temperature, such as 85 F (30 degrees Celsius), making sure that it doesn't come into direct contact with the heat. Cold smoking is mainly used

- **ROASTING SMOKE:** This is also known as Smoke Baking. This process is essentially a combined form of roasting and baking and can be performed in any smoker with a capacity to reach temperatures above 180 F (80 degrees Celsius).

SELECTING A SMOKER

You need to invest in a good smoker if you smoke meat regularly. Consider these options when buying a smoker. Here are two natural fire options for you:

- **CHARCOAL SMOKERS**: are fueled by a combination of charcoal and wood. Charcoal burns quickly, and the temperature remains steady so you won't have any problem with a charcoal smoker. The wood gives a great flavor to the meat, and you will enjoy smoking meat.
- **WOOD SMOKER:** The wood smoker will give your brisket and ribs the best smoky flavor and taste, but it is harder to cook with wood. Both hardwood blocks and chips are used as fuel.

DIFFERENT SMOKER TYPES

You should know that in the market, you will get three different types of Smokers

CHARCOAL SMOKER

These smokers are hands down the best for infusing the perfect smoky flavor to your meat. But be warned that these smokers are difficul2t to master as the method of regulating temperature is a little bit difficult compared to standard Gas or Electric smokers.

ELECTRIC SMOKER

After the charcoal smoker, next comes the more straightforward option, Electric Smokers. These are easy-to-use and plug-and-play types. All you need to do is plug in, set the temperature, and go about your daily life. The smoker will do the rest. However, remember that the smoky finishing flavor won't be as intense as the Charcoal one.

GAS SMOKERS

Finally, comes the Gas Smokers. These have a reasonably easy temperature control mechanism and are usually powered by LP Gas. The drawback of these Smokers is that you will have to keep checking up on your smoker now and then

to ensure that it has enough Gas.

DIFFERENT SMOKER STYLES

The different styles of Smokers are essentially divided into the following.

VERTICAL (BULLET STYLE USING CHARCOAL)

These are usually low-cost solutions and are perfect for first-time smokers.

VERTICAL (CABINET STYLE)

These Smokers have a square-shaped design with cabinets and drawers/trays for easy accessibility. These cookers come with a water tray and a designated wood chips box.

OFFSET

These types of smokers have dedicated fireboxes that are attached to the side of the main grill. The smoke and heat required for these are generated from the firebox, which is passed through the main chamber and out through a nicely placed chimney.

KAMADO JOE

And finally, we have the Kamado Joe, which ceramic smokers are largely regarded as being the "Jack of All Trades." These smokers can be used as low and slow smokers, grills, high or low-temperature ovens, and so on.

They have a thick ceramic wall that allows them to hold heat better than any other smoker, requiring only a little charcoal.

These are easy to use with better insulation and are more efficient when it comes to fuel control.

comes to fuel control.

CHOOSE YOUR WOOD

You need to choose your wood carefully because the type of wood you will use affect significantly to the flavor and taste of the meat. Here are a few options for you:

- **MAPLE**: Maple has a smoky and sweet taste and goes well with pork or poultry
- **ALDER**: Alder is sweet and light. Perfect for poultry and fish.
- **APPLE**: Apple has a mild and sweet flavor. Goes well with pork, fish, and poultry.
- **OAK**: Oak is great for slow cooking. Ideal for game, pork, beef, and lamb.
- **MESQUITE**: Mesquite has a smoky flavor and is extremely strong. Goes well with pork or beef.
- **HICKORY**: Has a smoky and strong flavor. Goes well with beef and lamb.
- **CHERRY**: Has a mild and sweet flavor. Great for pork, beef, and turkey

The Different Types Of Wood	Suitable For
Hickory	Wild game, chicken, pork, cheeses, beef
Pecan	Chicken, pork, lamb, cheeses, fish.
Mesquite	Beef and vegetables
Alder	Swordfish, Salmon, Sturgeon and other types of fishes. Works well with pork and chicken too.
Oak	Beef or briskets
Maple	Vegetable, ham or poultry
Cherry	Game birds, poultry or pork
Apple	Game birds, poultry, beef
Peach	Game birds, poultry or pork
Grape Vines	Beef, chicken or turkey
Wine Barrel Chips	Turkey, beef, chicken or cheeses
Seaweed	Lobster, mussels, crab, shrimp etc.
Herbs or Spices such as rosemary, bay leaves, mint, lemon peels, whole nutmeg etc.	Good for cheeses or vegetables and a small collection of light meats such as fillets or fish steaks.

In General, there are three different types of charcoal. All of them are porous residues of black color made of carbon and ashes. However, the following are a little distinguishable due to their specific features.

- **BBQ BRIQUETTES:** These are the ones that are made from a fine blend of charcoal and char.

- **CHARCOAL BRIQUETTES:** These are created by compressing charcoal and are made from sawdust or wood products.

- **LUMP CHARCOAL**: These are made directly from hardwood and are the most premium quality charcoals. They are entirely natural and are free from any form of additives.

RIGHT TEMPERATURE

- Start at 250F (120C): Start your smoker a bit hot. This extra heat gets the smoking process going.

- Temperature drop: Once you add the meat to the smoker, the temperature will drop, which is fine.

- Maintain the temperature. Monitor and maintain the temperature. Keep the temperature steady during the smoking process.

Avoid peeking now and then. Smoke and heat are the two crucial elements that make your meat taste great. If you open the cover every now, and then you lose both of them, and your meat loses flavor. Only open the lid only when you truly need it.

BASIC PREPARATIONS

- Always be prepared to spend the whole day and take as much time as possible to smoke your meat for maximum effect.
- Ensure you obtain the perfect Ribs/Meat for the meal you are trying to smoke. Do a little bit of research if you need.
- I have already added a list of woods. Consult that list and choose the perfect wood for your meal.
- Make sure to prepare the marinade for each of the meals properly. A great deal of the flavors comes from the rubbing.
- Keep a meat thermometer handy to get the internal temperature when needed.
- Use mittens or tongs to keep yourself safe.
- Please refrain from using charcoal infused alongside starter fluid, as it might bring a very unpleasant odor to your food.
- Always start with a small amount of wood and keep adding them as you cook.
- Don't be afraid to experiment with different types of wood for newer flavors and experiences.
- Always keep a notebook near you and note jot down whatever you are doing or learning and use them during future sessions. A notebook will help you to evolve and move forward.

ELEMENTS OF SMOKING

Smoking is a very indirect method of cooking that relies on many factors to give you the most perfectly cooked meal you are looking for. Each component is essential to the whole process as they all work together to create the meal of your dreams.

- **TIME**: Unlike grilling or even Barbequing, smoking takes a long time and requires a lot of patience. It takes time for the smoky flavor to get infused into the meats slowly. Just to compare things, it takes about 8 minutes to thoroughly cook a steak through direct heating, while smoking (indirect heating) will take around 35-40 minutes.

- **TEMPERATURE:** When it comes to smoking, the temperature is affected by many factors that are not only limited to the wind and cold air temperatures but also the cooking wood's dryness. Some smokers work best with large fires that are controlled by the draw of a chimney and restricted airflow through the various vents of the cooking chamber and firebox. At the same time, other smokers tend to require minor fire with fewer coals and a completely different combination of the vent and draw controls. However, most smokers are designed to work at temperatures as low as 180 degrees Fahrenheit to as high as 300 degrees Fahrenheit. But the recommended temperature usually falls between 250 degrees Fahrenheit and 275 degrees Fahrenheit.

- **AIRFLOW**: The air to which the fire is significantly exposed determines how your fire will burn and how quickly it will burn the fuel. For instance, if you restrict airflow into the firebox by closing up the available vents, the fire will burn at a low temperature and vice versa. Typically in smokers, after lighting up the fire, the vents are opened to allow for maximum airflow and are then adjusted throughout the cooking process to ensure that optimum flame is achieved.

- **INSULATION:** Insulation is also essential for smokers as it helps to manage the cooking process throughout the whole cooking session. Good insulation allows smokers to reach the desired temperature instead of waiting hours!

SAFETY

CLEANLINESS OF THE MEAT

If you can follow the steps below, you will be able to ensure that your meat is safe from any bacterial or airborne contamination.

This first step is essential as no market-bought or freshly cut meat is entirely sterile.

Following these would significantly minimize the risk of getting affected by diseases.

- Make sure to properly wash your hands before beginning to process your meat. Use fresh tap water and soap/hand sanitizer.
- Make sure to remove metal ornaments such as rings and watches from your wrist and hand before handling the meat.
- Thoroughly clean the cutting surface using sanitizing liquid to remove any grease or unwanted contaminants. If you want a homemade sanitizer, you can simply make a solution of 1 part chlorine bleach and ten parts water.
- The sanitizer mentioned above should also be used to soak your tools, such as knives and other equipment, to ensure that they are safe to use.
- Alternatively, commercial acid based/ no rinsed sanitizers such as Star San will also work.
- After each use, all knives and other equipment, such as meat grinders, slicers, extruders, etc., should be cleaned thoroughly using soap water. The knives should be taken care in particular by cleaning the place just on top of the handle as it might contain blood and pieces of meat.
- When cleaning the surface, you should use cloths or sponges.

A note of sponges/clothes: It is ideal that you keep your sponge or cleaning cloth clean as it might result in cross-contamination. These are ideal harboring places for foodborne pathogens. Just follow the simple steps to ensure that you are on the safe side:

- Make sure to clean your sponge daily. It is seen that the effectiveness of cleaning it increases if you microwave the dam sponge for 1 minute and disinfect it using a solution of ¼ -1/2 teaspoon of concentrated bleach. This process will kill 99% of bacteria.
- Replace your sponge frequently, as using the same sponge every time (even with wash) will result in eventual bacterial growth.
- When not using the sponge, please keep it dry and wring it off of any loose food or debris.

KEEPING YOUR MEAT COLD

Mismanagement of temperature is one of the most common reasons for outbreaks of foodborne diseases. The study has shown that bacteria grow best at temperatures of 40 to 140 degree Fahrenheit/4-60 degree Celsius, which means that if not taken care of properly, bacteria in the meat will start to multiply very quickly. The best way to prevent this is to keep your meat cold before using it. Keep them eat in your fridge before processing them and make sure that the temperature is below 40 degrees Fahrenheit/4 degree Celsius.

KEEPING YOUR MEAT COVERED

All foods start to diminish once they are opened from their packaging or exposed to the air. However, the effect can be greatly minimized if you cover or wrap the foods properly.

The same goes for meat.

Good ways of keeping your meat covered and wrapped include:

- Using aluminum foil to cover up your meat will help to protect it from light and oxygen and keep the moisture intact. However, since Aluminum is reactive, it is advised that a layer of plastic wrap is used underneath the aluminum foil to provide a double protective coating.
- If the meat is kept in a bowl with no lid, then plastic wrap can seal the bowl, providing an airtight enclosure.
- Re-sealable bags protect by storing them in a bag and squeezing out any air.
- Airtight glass or plastic containers with lids are good options as well.
- A type of paper known as Freezer paper is specifically designed to wrap foods to be kept in the fridge. These wraps are excellent for meat as well.
- Vacuum sealers are often used for Sous Vide packaging. These machines are a bit expensive but can provide excellent packaging by completely sucking out any air from a re-sealable bag. This greatly increases the meat's shelf life outside and in the fridge.

PREVENTING FORMS OF CROSS-CONTAMINATION

Cross-Contamination usually occurs when one food comes into contact with another. In our case, we are talking about our meats.

This can be avoided very easily by keeping the following things in check:

- Always wash your hands thoroughly with warm water. The cutting boards, counters, knives, and other utensils should also be cleaned as instructed in the chapter's first section.
- Keep different types of meat in separate bowls, dishes, and plates before using them.
- When storing the meat in the fridge, keep the raw meat, seafood, poultry, and eggs on the bottom shelf of your fridge and in individual sealed containers.
- Keep your refrigerator shelves cleaned, and juices from meat/vegetables might drip on them.
- Always refrain from keeping raw meat/vegetables on the same plate as cooked goods.
- Always clean your cutting boards and use different cutting boards for different foods. Raw meats, vegetables, and other foods should be cut using a different table.

KNIVES

KNIVES: Sharp knives should be used to slice the meat accordingly. While using the knife, you should keep the following in mind.

- Always make sure to use a sharp knife
- Never hold a knife under your arm or leave it under a piece of meat
- Always keep your knives within visible distance
- Always keep your knife point down
- Always cut down towards the cutting surface and away from your body
- Never allow children to toy with knives unattended
- Wash the knives while cutting different types of food

CONCLUSION

I am happy to share this cookbook with you, and I take pride in offering you an extensive array of recipes that you will love and enjoy. I hope you benefit from each of our recipes, and I am sure you will like all the recipes we have offered you. Don't hesitate to try our creative and easy-to-make recipes, and remember that I have put my heart into coming up with delicious meals for you. If you like my recipes, you can share them with acquaintances and friends. I need your encouragement to continue writing more books!

P.S. Thank you for reading this book. If you've enjoyed this book, please don't shy; drop me a line, leave feedback, or both on Amazon. I love reading feedback and your opinion is extremely important to me.

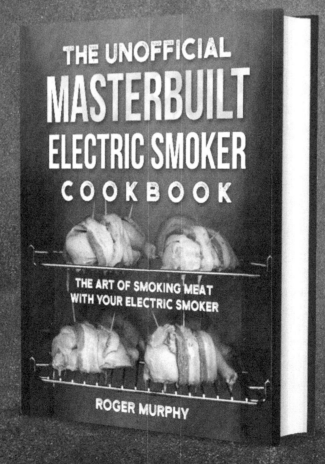

THE UNOFFICIAL
MASTERBUILT
ELECTRIC SMOKER
COOKBOOK

THE ART OF SMOKING MEAT
WITH YOUR ELECTRIC SMOKER

ROGER MURPHY

Made in the USA
Las Vegas, NV
08 November 2023

80435372R00111